Tales from the Simpson Literary Project

SIMP SONI STAS

VOL. 3

Edited by Joseph Di Prisco

Tales from the Simpson Literary Project

SIMP SONI STAS

VOL. 3

EDITED BY JOSEPH DI PRISCO

*Dedicated to the memory of
Charlie Gross (1936–2019)
Father of cognitive neuroscience, professor,
photographer, adventurer.*

Contents

NOTES & ACKNOWLEDGMENTS

Grateful thanks extended to

Authors and publishers for generous permission to print or reprint.

Original, previously unpublished work printed with permission of the authors.

"The Winter Soldier" (excerpt from the novel *The Winter Soldier*), Daniel Mason. Reprinted with permission of the author and Little, Brown.

"The Second Doctor Service," Daniel Mason. Previously published in *Harper's* and in *A Registry of My Passage Upon the Earth*. Reprinted with permission of the author and Little, Brown.

"Q&A with Daniel Mason": Regan McMahon. Originally published in *Zyzzyva*. Reprinted with permission of the authors.

"Mastiff," Joyce Carol Oates. Originally published in *The New Yorker*. Reprinted with permission of the author.

"Two Poems," Joyce Carol Oates. "The Tunnel" and "Palliative" reprinted with permission of the author.

"Four Poems," Noah Warren. "Cut Lilies," "If We Are to Go Forward," "Automatic Pool Cleaner," and "Across from the Winter Palace" appeared in *The Destroyer in the Glass*, Yale Series of Younger Poets, Yale University Press. Reprinted with permission of the author.

"Early Morning Thoughts on Ahab," Peter Orner. Printed with permission of the author.

"Atitlán," Peter Orner. Originally published in *Zyzzyva*. Reprinted with permission of the author.

"The Mere Wife" (excerpt from the novel *The Mere Wife*), Maria Dahvana Headley. Reprinted with permission of MCD/FSG and the author.

"That Time at My Brother's Wedding," Laila Lalami. Originally appeared in the *New York Times Magazine*, reprinted with permission of the author.

Post-(Movie)-Script: *Shakespeare & the Plague*: Philippa Kelly & Joseph Di Prisco. Reprinted with permission of the authors.

Thank you.

PEOPLE, PLACES, & THINGS

Simpson Project Writing Workshops—

Contra Costa County Juvenile Hall, Martinez, California; Noelle Burch, Contra Costa County Public Library; Mt. McKinley High School, Contra Costa County Office of Education; Brian Murtagh, Assistant Principal. Robert Bowers, Principal.

2020 workshops cancelled due to pandemic; virtual workshop scheduled to resume Spring 2021.

Girls Inc., Alameda County; Julayne Virgil, CEO; Gabi Reyes-Acosta, Jazmin Noble, Aja Holland, Carina Silva. https://girlsinc-alameda.org/

Two virtual workshops scheduled in Spring 2021.

Northgate High School, Mount Diablo Unified School District; David Wood, faculty. https://northgatehighschool.org/

Virtual workshop scheduled in Spring 2021.

Cal Prep. The Richmond Aspire California College Preparatory Academy (Cal Prep) is a public charter and early college secondary school, cofounded by University of California, Berkeley, and Aspire Public Schools. Tatiana Lim-Breitbart, Principal.

Virtual workshop scheduled in Spring 2021.

Simpson Fellows: Workshop Leaders 2017–2020
University of California, Berkeley, English Department—

Uttara Chintamani Chaudhuri

Frank Cruz

Katherine Ding

Lise Gaston

John James

Ismail Muhammad

Laura Ritland

Rosetta Young

Noah Warren

Joyce Carol Oates Prize

Awarded annually, $50,000, not to a book, but to a distinguished
mid-career author, one who has emerged and is still emerging.

2021 Joyce Carol Oates Prize Finalists

Danielle Evans

Jenny Offill

Darin Strauss

Lysley Tenorio

(Recipient named May 2021)

2020 Joyce Carol Oates Prize Finalists

Chris Bachelder

Maria Dahvana Headley

Rebecca Makkai

Daniel Mason (Prize Recipient)

Peter Orner

Dexter Palmer

Kevin Wilson

2019 Simpson/Joyce Carol Oates Prize Finalists

Rachel Kushner

Laila Lalami (Prize Recipient)

Valeria Luiselli

Sigrid Nunez

Anne Raeff

Amor Towles

2018 Simpson/Joyce Carol Oates Prize Finalists

Ben Fountain

Samantha Hunt

Karan Mahajan

Anthony Marra (Prize Recipient)

Martin Pousson

2017 Simpson/Joyce Carol Oates Prize Finalists

    T. Geronimo Johnson (Prize Recipient)

    Valeria Luiselli

    Lori Ostlund

    Dana Spiotta

Joyce Carol Prize Longlisted Authors' Publishers 2017, 2018, 2019, 2020, 2021
(with number of their authors listed):

    Algonquin (5)

    Back Bay (1)

    Bellevue Literary (3)

    Bloomsbury (5)

    Catapult (2)

    Coffee House (1)

    Counterpoint (10)

    Delphinium (1)

    Dial (2)

    Doubleday (4)

    Dutton (1)

    Dzanc (1)

    Ecco (16)

    Elixir (1)

    Flatiron (1)

    FSG (13)

    Grand Central (1)

    Graywolf (5)

    Grove (4)

    Harper Collins (3) (2017 Prize Recipient)

    Hogarth (2) (2018 Prize Recipient)

    HoughtonMiflin (4)

    Knopf (8)

Little Brown (13) (2020 Prize Recipient)

Mariner (1)

MCD/FSG (2)

Melville House (1)

Nan A. Talese (1)

Norton (7)

Pantheon (1) (2019 Prize Recipient)

Penguin (11)

Picador (2)

Putnam (5)

Random House (6)

Rare Bird (2)

Riverhead (19)

Simon Schuster (5)

Soft Skull (1)

Soho (4)

St. Martin (4)

Tim Duggan (1)

Tin House (1)

Viking (6)

2021 Joyce Carol Oates Prize: Longlisted Authors by Current Publisher

BELLEVUE LITERARY

Andrew Krivak

Norman Lock

DELPHINIUM

Jessica Treadway

ECCO

Rumaan Alam

Debra Jo Immergut

Ivy Pochoda

Lysley Tenorio

Laura Zigman

FSG

Marie-Helene Bertino

Sarah Shun-lien Bynum

Garth Greenwell

Catherine Lacey

Laura Van Den Berg

GRAND CENTRAL

Leesa Cross-Smith

GREYWOLF

Percival Everett

Ander Monson

KNOPF

Yaa Gyasi

Jenny Offill

Rufi Thorpe

MCD/FSG

Hector Tobar

PUTNAM

Chloe Benjamin

Courtney Maum

RANDOM HOUSE

Téa Obreht

Darin Strauss

RIVERHEAD

Britt Bennett

Blake Butler

Danielle Evans

Jacqueline Woodson

Lidia Yuknavitch

SIMON & SCHUSTER

Micheline Aharonian Marcom

Jurors (Rotated Yearly) for the Joyce Carol Oates Prize 2017, 2018, 2019, 2020, 2021:

Heidi Benson

Anne Cain

Joseph Di Prisco, Chair

Professor Joshua Gang

Professor Donna Jones

Regan McMahon

Professor Geoffrey O'Brien

Professor Katherine Snyder

David Wood

Professor Dora Zhang

Deep gratitude to the awesome Vickie Sciacca, of the Lafayette Library

and Learning Center, for kindly, expert coordination.

Final Judges for the Joyce Carol Oates Prize:

Project Board

Diane Del Signore, Executive Director, Simpson Literary Project
diane@simpsonliteraryproject.org

Joseph Di Prisco, Chair, Author & Educator jdp@simpsonliteraryproject.org

Shanti Ariker, Attorney

Steven Justice, English Professor, Chair of the English Department, University of California, Berkeley

Beth Needel, Executive Director, Lafayette Library and Learning Center Foundation

Joyce Carol Oates (Honorary), Author and Professor of Humanities, Princeton University

Genaro Padilla, Chair Emeritus, English Department; Vice Chancellor Emeritus, University of California, Berkeley

Michael Ross, Retired Attorney and Author

Pat Scott, Public Radio and Nonprofit Executive

Frank Starn, Community Leader and Corporate Executive

David Wood, Community Leader and Public High School English Teacher, Northgate High School, Walnut Creek, CA

Project Team

Diane Del Signore, Executive Director | diane@simpsonliteraryproject.org

Tyson Cornell, Publicist & Publicity Rare Bird | tyson@rarebirdlit.com

Josephine Courant, Digital Design

Ashley Pattison-Scott, Lead Digital Strategist

Institutional Partners of the Simpson Literary Project

The Lafayette Library and Learning Center Foundation, fiscal sponsor (2017-). lllcf.org/

The University of California, Berkeley, English Department. english.berkeley.edu/

The University of California, Berkeley. berkeley.edu/

The Simpson Literary Project

With abundant, humble gratitude for the generous donors who make possible the nonprofit Simpson Literary Project: https://www.simpsonliteraryproject.org/about

PREFACE:

JOURNAL OF OUR PLAGUE YEAR:

SIMPSON LITERARY PROJECT

OCTOBER 2019–NOVEMBER 2020

"Being
Observations or Memorials,
Of the most remarkable
OCCURRENCES,
as well
PUBLICK as PRIVATE,
Which happened in [The United States]
During the last
GREAT VISITATION
In [2020].
Written by a CITIZEN who continued all the while in [California].
Never made publick before"

Apologies to the redoubtable Daniel Defoe. I take liberties in my epigraph, emending the title page of his remarkable novel-as-journalism *A Journal of the Plague Year*. Published in 1722, his book gives an account of London's "last great visitation" of 1655, which occurred when the author happened to be five. That historical delimitation doesn't diminish Defoe's haunting, unyielding, cold-eyed depiction of the terror, when twenty-five percent of the city's population perished.

Since our own last great visitation in the United States, the 2020-21 COVID-19 pandemic, the communal sense of fear, loss, restriction, anxiety, dread, boredom, and disruption has deepened and deepened by the day. Perhaps at some point you dusted off Defoe's book along with Albert Camus's *The Plague*—in pursuit of solace, edification, or distraction. If you couldn't locate the texts on your bookshelves, the local library likely proved impervious to public access, and bookstores were shuttered as well, deemed inessential. Online book marketers enjoyed a field day, but the blessings of their business plan were decidedly mixed as far as the macro-economy and the average consumer were concerned (more on that later).

Your book group or your class may have huddled together in cyberspace, because everybody fast became a Zoom zealot. That's an intriguing tech development with mind-warping consequence for commercial real estate, office space, public transportation, highway repair, airline travel, and, I don't know, everything else including tequila tasting, flirting, birthday celebrating, couples' counseling, worshipping, job interviewing, car purchase negotiating (though who needed a car?). All the same, people, being social creatures, stressed over how to appear before their computer camera or how to set-design their personal space. It was all virtual, 24/7. But since Zooming makes it hard to read people absent body language signals, who knows what was missed or misconstrued in the interchanges? Nevertheless, Zoom stock soared and lessons were learned. (*People, you need to unmute. No, wait, everybody, mute yourself! Hey, you can't eat a burrito, especially while unmuted and checking your email. We can hear you. Oh, and that creature on your lap is an adorable... Malamute? Wolf?*) And almost before we knew it, we thought we were Zoomed out. But then, wait a minute, maybe not so fast.

After shouldering day after day, night after night, the psychological, emotional, political weight of this pandemic, you may have felt persistently exhausted. I myself have found it hard to concentrate, even long after I was waylaid for five weeks with what I'm convinced was a very mild bout with the bug (for which my medical provider was not able to test me in March or April, which is another story; the most advanced health delivery system in the world, the United States of America's, proved anemic when it came to testing and tracing—as it continues to be). I'm no long-hauler, thankfully, and I have recovered with no residual aftereffects as far as I know, except for whatever evidence may be detected in these pages, thanks for asking. At this point, I could hasten to assure you "Enough about me," but I am just getting started.

The great and not-so-great, the emerging as well as the emerged writers alike will doubtless take their shot at illuminating what has become of our reality, at plumbing the pandemic's depths, implications, and ramifications. My aspiration here is more limited. I simply seek to take snapshots, and show what I believe to be this great visitation's impact upon the nonprofit Simpson Literary Project, by which I mean upon our communities of writers, readers, and students. I will fail, I am confident, to do justice to that subject—because it turns out to be not such a limited aspiration after all. For us on the ground the experience has been apocalyptic. Consider the root metaphor: apocalypse means *uncovering*. Yes, we've been uncovered, stripped of our illusions and disabused of our presumptions. It shouldn't have constituted late-breaking news, but in the end we refamiliarized ourselves with how precious little of our lives lies within our control—the penultimate bubble to burst in the vainglorious pursuit of wisdom. Because each of us is living our own pandemic, as is every writer and every teacher and every observer, as is every one of our readers, as is every arts and literary community, perforce the account must be personal. All the while keeping in mind that the "good man," as Camus's narrator famously attests in *The Plague*, "has the fewest lapses of attention."

Once upon a time, in what feels like a prelapsarian epoch, the Simpson Literary Project (SLP) was a brazen little startup nonprofit with outsize, bold ideas about readers and reading, writers and writing, teaching and learning, literature and literacy, community and responsibility, opportunity and obligation. Nobody ever regarded us as shy and unassuming. Then the pandemic came along and singled us out for special attention. Now to be fair, it singled out everyone and everything everywhere for special attention. While COVID-19 had designs on devastating the human species, it also took our enterprise along for a diabolical spin. Once inside the physical body, the outer spike—the corona—of the virus latches onto receptors in the respiratory tract, the ACE2 receptors, and insidiously sets about to do the rest of its dirty work in other major organs as well. Insinuating itself inside our Project, the virus seeks to latch onto our social and intellectual and artistic receptors and do something wickedly similar: to take away our institutional capacity to breathe and our ability to survive as an organization with our mission.

Here I recall that gallows funny/not so funny moment in Joseph Heller's *Catch-22*:

"They're trying to kill me," Yossarian told him calmly.

"No one's trying to kill you," Clevinger cried.

"Then why are they shooting at me?" Yossarian asked.

"They're shooting at everyone," Clevinger answered. "They're trying to kill everyone."

"And what difference does that make?"

~

Black lives matter. Nobody needs a transition anymore. Time's up for transitions. Black lives matter. We cannot say that often enough, forcefully enough. Now if only we could understand and then live up to the conviction. Systemic racism and health care inequities make Blacks more vulnerable to COVID-19. From early on, research indisputably confirmed the virus wreaks disproportionate damage on communities of color.

~

Throughout this ordeal, I look for every opportunity to quote William Butler Yeats:

All changed, changed utterly:

A terrible beauty is born.

Of course, that is the poet's resigned, heroic, plangent refrain in "Easter 1918," considered by many one of the greatest political poems ever composed—but if pressed I could also delete the qualifier "one of" as well as "political," and be good with that, too. His haunting lines raise a question. Here I am in the last days of Fall 2020, the holiday season upon us, and all seems changed, changed utterly. Will any sort of terrible beauty be born?

People are cracking up all around, and sometimes some of them are me. The pandemics are savagely converging: viral, economic, social, racial, political, existential. John Cage was once imprudently asked if there was too much suffering in the world, and he replied: "No, just the right amount." That wisecrack normally (what train did *normally* take out of town?) speaks to a hard truth I accept, if begrudgingly. But what about these days? Too glib? Too soon? Too late? Susan Sontag wrote brilliantly about "illness as metaphor." Does the experience of this pandemic—these contagions—render inoperable the longing to cross over into metaphor? Sontag as per usual beat us to the punch: "The most truthful way of regarding illness—and the healthiest way of being ill—is one most purified of, most resistant to, metaphoric thinking." It's the brute facticity of the pandemic that bowls us over again and again. The escalating number of deaths. The abject corruption. The political deceitfulness. The hideous lunacy. The tragic poverty. The systemic racism. The cultural divisions. The loss. The loss. The loss.

How about this for a nice coincidence that isn't very nice at all? More than a few followers of SLP called attention to a certain, unintentionally "prophetic" passage in my introduction to *Simpsonistas: Tales from the Simpson Literary Project Vol. 2*, published in Fall 2019. At that juncture, I had been struck sensible by a practically anthemic piece by pseudonymous Elena Ferrante celebrating women's storytelling: "Storytelling, in other words, gives us the power to bring order to the chaos of the real under our own sign, and in this it isn't very far from political power" ("A Power of Our Own"; *The New York Times*, 5/18/2019). In the course of the essay, the author references *The Decameron*, which has by now assumed totemic, if not monumental status in literate discussion, but back then, emboldened in the pre-times, I was off and running:

...[I]n the precarious 21st century, dystopian visions proliferate. Ferrante's op-ed... references brilliantly the 14th century author, Giovanni Boccaccio, who wrote a great book called The Decameron. *Ten young people flee Florence for the countryside. In the city, chaos has broken out—citizens are in abject panic over the plague, in fear of their neighbors and friends and family. And these ten storytellers converge to do something quite radical and ultimately sensible: they compose and tell each other over ten days a hundred stories of love and lust and adventure and heroism. (As Ferrante trenchantly points out, seven of the ten storytellers are women.) In his book's first line he writes: "Umana cosa è aver compassione degli afflitti." That is, it is (an essentially) human (thing) to have compassion for those in distress. But how to express compassion, sympathy, empathy under such dire circumstances? For Boccaccio, it was to tell and attend to stories. History and literature have proven him and his book prescient. Storytelling*

is not an escape from the grimmest realities, but the subtly shifting, fluid foundation of our mutual humanity, which stories are uniquely positioned to illuminate—and fashion (p. 12).

Upon reflection, I'll have to agree with myself.

So yeah, but no, I am no Nostradamus. (That overrated seer's track record as detailed in the *Racing Form* of legend is unimpressive anyway.) As for my prescience, my son still claims I predicted back in the day that rap music would never catch on. I contest this scurrilous imputation. But I need to go back to what Ferrante wrote about storytelling, how it brings "order out of chaos." Has storytelling today accomplished that task? How would we know once, or if, it did? And when would we know it? And always the essential smack-in-the-mouth question: who exactly is this *we*?

~

It feels like the wheels are coming off. Raise your hands if you haven't felt surges of anxiety. If you did raise your hand, sorry, I don't believe you, and if I did, I would harbor my suspicions. And as the University of California, Berkeley, Chancellor, the inspirational Carol Christ, memorably wrote last summer to the university community: "I must also acknowledge a fundamental truth: The pandemic has highlighted deep racial and socioeconomic disparities on our campus and beyond. We may be in the same storm, but we are not in the same boat." The one-percenters, and especially the uber-wealthy, profited spectacularly, though almost everyone else has been financially bludgeoned. The fault lines of our economy have deepened. The poor got poorer. People lost jobs, their homes. Food became rampantly insecure. To this day, unemployment is soaring. This is a recession, verging on a depression. Small businesses are foundering and Small Business Administration money is not saving the day. Schools cannot open or stay that way long—and who knows what physiological, emotional, intellectual price students and society at large will ultimately pay for lost time and opportunity to learn in community? It threatens to be exorbitant. Wearing a mask has become in some quarters the most cravenly and idiotically politicized cause célèbre. Free not to wear a mask? Free not to chance infecting others? Free to walk pantsless into the grocery store? Free to drive inebriated or without wearing a seatbelt? Unabashed, arrogant, reckless, and loony libertarianism runs amok.

Forgive me for wondering for a fleeting moment, however, in the interests of due diligence: Dare we glimpse any silver linings? (FYI: Board chairs managing for organizational stress are hard-wired to search for silver linings.) The binary question points to a disaster in and of itself, with (as I write this) a million dead worldwide and over three hundred thousand, and counting and counting and counting, in the United States, with fifteen million infected. In what regard has our world *not* been shaken? Name one field of endeavor *not* radically upended. And here's another, related question that pops up incessantly: When will life return to what it was? The answer becomes clearer all the time: Never. As Dr. Siddhartha Mukherjee wrote: "When will things get back to normal? But, as a physician and researcher, I fear that the resumption of normality would signal a failure to learn. We need to think not about resumption but about revision" (*The New Yorker*, 4 May 2020). What exactly is it that we might fail to learn?

Which is not a novel question, not if you recall Thucydides' fifth century BCE account in *The History of the Peloponnesian Wars* of the Athens plague that arrived in the summer of 430 BCE, which perhaps was an outbreak of typhus: "All speculation as to its origin and its causes, if causes can be found adequate to produce so great a disturbance, I leave to other writers, whether lay or professional; for myself, I shall simply set down its nature, and explain the symptoms by which perhaps it may be recognized by the student, if it should ever break out again. This I can the better do, as I had the disease myself, and watched its operation in the case of others" (Rex Warner, translator).

With maybe some thoughts relevant to COVID-deniers: "So they resolved to spend quickly and enjoy themselves, regarding their lives and riches as alike things of a day. Perseverance in what men called honor was popular with none, it was so uncertain whether they would be spared to attain the object; but it was settled that present enjoyment, and all that contributed to it, was both honorable and useful. Fear of gods or law of man there was none to restrain them."

Reducing to what? "The strong do what they can and the weak suffer what they must."

And in the end what does this tell us about the human species and the role of the self-nominated writer? "Besides, I know the Athenian character from experience: you like to be told pleasant news, but if things do not turn out in the way you have been led to expect, then you blame your informants afterward. I therefore thought it safer to let you know the truth."

~

During *annus horribilis* 2020, the world has been infected by contagion, inflamed by political and racial outrage, and wracked by social tensions and also, here in California, catastrophic wildfires that incinerated lives and livelihoods and befouled the very air we choked on. Not to mention murder hornets. I'll leave it there. Just, murder hornets. But also, I guess, TikTok. And what is it with people fracturing their teeth in unprecedented numbers and the widespread TMJ suffering? Stresses, anxieties, fears are abounding. And TikTok, too.

Nonprofits, in particular all those literary and educational nonprofits whose work is tangentially related to SLP's, are facing the prospect of mass extinction. The equivalent of an asteroid has smashed into our world. Put simply, fundraising is in grave jeopardy, and the common sense, moral question seizes donors by the collar: Why support the arts—theater, poetry, music, museums, literature, and so on—when people need food and shelter, and when social injustice implicates and ravages communities, and when all the pandemics—viral, social, political, existential—converge? Is there a hierarchy of needs? (*Paging Professor Maslow. Professor Maslow?*) Yes, indeed there certainly is. But then there's this. The short version of the complex response to that question is: Both/And. We desperately need art to remind us of, and to reaffirm and express, our humanity. We need storytelling and storytellers. Writers and readers and teachers. Is there a hierarchy of needs? Yes. But when I say fundraising is in jeopardy, what that means is writers and readers and students and teachers are suffering as a result. As Toni Morrison once wrote:

This is precisely the time when artists go to work…. I know the world is bruised and bleeding, and though it is important not to ignore its pain, it is also critical to refuse to succumb to its malevolence. Like failure, chaos contains information that can lead to knowledge—even wisdom. Like art.

We embrace the challenges. Because? Because we have no choice. But in a more immediate, intensified sense, with the Simpson Literary Project, we have come to terms with our limits, our mortality. And that's a bracing, essential step. We're not sure of anything except of our inability to predict the future. And yet, we go forward. Sobering as the news is, this all must sound familiar to any serious writer. A novel, a story, a poem, a memoir, a play—all fleeting stays against mortality. What is more preposterous than exercising one's imagination in the honest work of making art? In the words of the great poet and physician from New Jersey, William Carlos Williams:

> It is difficult
> to get the news from poems
> > yet men die miserably every day
> > > for lack
> of what is found there.

~

Black lives matter. That's still the news.

~

In the early days of March 2020 moments before the pandemic became all too real, the SLP board spent one whole day putting the finishing touches on our Strategic Plan, which we had been working on for months. Trust me, it looked great, you would have been impressed. We had come so far in four short years. More than that, in a true sense we had *arrived*, taken our place on the stage. Man, we had ambitions. We had the confidence to go forward and the financial wherewithal, too. Plans, yeah *plans*, pretty comical to contemplate now, right?

Then in the aftermath, when quarantines and lockdowns kicked in, many of our programs, and pretty much all of our revenue-generating designs that served in the past, went up in smoke. It was darkness at noon. So we had choices to make. In the image captured by Frank Starn, Finance Chair of SLP: We decided we were not going to sit on the beach, and we were not going to tread water, either. We were going to see if we could get to the other side of the lake. It looked sublime over there, and we would go for it. And in place of our marvelous strategic plan and led by our Executive Director, Diane Del Signore, we conceived three new, not exactly plans but, three pathways to—more than survive—thrive, maybe not immediately, but someday:

Improvise—*on the fly, if not before.*
Make mistakes—*no risk, no reward.*
Think magically—*hey, maybe this is just crazy enough to work.*

I'm no Master of Business Administration, but I have sat on and chaired enough nonprofit boards in the company of many a shiny MBA (like Frank, Chicago, and Diane, Stanford) to acknowledge those pathways do indeed sound absolutely batshit anathema. You know the kind of person to whom such pathways are *not* batshit anathema? Artists. If a writer isn't ready to make mistakes (that is, to take risks, many of which must inevitably fail), and if a writer isn't prepared to imagine the incredibility, the improbability of making art, then I don't know what they are doing in the first place. And as any actor and comedian would testify, the key to improvisation is never saying No, always saying Yes. SLP says Yes.

Let us factor in the Simpson Literary Project experience as perceived upon the ground we once upon a time took for granted as we used to tread maskless and sometimes arm in arm, when we lifted a glass in good cheer without giving a thought to a virus that wanted to take our breath away, and not breathless in the good way as with a great work of art. Uttara Chintamani Chaudhuri, Simpson Fellow at Girls Inc.-Alameda County and Berkeley English Department stellar grad student, collaborated with the sterling organization staff, working magic to bring her two virtual workshops to life with girls of color who aspire to be the first in their families to attend college, the first to publish a poem or story in a nationally distributed anthology, our *Simpsonistas*. Nobody can tell me that these girls' lives have not been changed, and changed utterly. I heard with my own two ears the mother of one of the girls from Girls Inc. after her daughter read at our annual celebration in 2019, and brought down the packed house at the Lafayette Public Library. Mom said, with eyes glistening and a smile, "She will never be the same."

On this score, Ms. Chaudhuri reflects on one of her students in the throes of the pandemic in the spring, and quoted in the brilliant essay on her teaching experience that is included in our anthology: "As one of my students said at the end of class, 'I feel less alone now. There's just something about knowing that someone else is going through what you are.'" About which sentiment—though it's more resonant, more resolute than mere sentiment—she directs this ray of illumination: "[M]y time with the scholars at Girls Inc. taught me that stories alone can defy, and always have defied, social distancing. Good stories foster radical empathy so that we can inhabit the minds and hearts of those far from us, even as they remind us of how much we have in common."

There it is. A not-so-terrible beauty is born, and reborn in every Simpson Literary Project workshop.

~

Time's a funny thing. It's also not so funny these days, though honestly when it's not so funny it can be downright hilarious. I've lost count of the number of people I heard testify that their dream lives have never been so lively. Maybe that's because the pandemic forces into consciousness as well as unconsciousness the comprehensive questions (how will we survive?) about our existence on earth (hey, people, climate change!), in other words our individual and collective mortalities. And it competes for attention with another urgent question: what shall I have for breakfast, and will it be green tea or coffee or Diet Coke? The mind reels. Because it does. A reel is a dance. In this case, excuse my French, a *danse macabre*. That was a pop sensation in the Middle Ages, when plagues were really *plagues*, or so we used to quaintly think. Remember the Middle Ages? A lot like the seventies, only without disco balls and with galumphing tumbrels and booming cries to *Bring out your dead!* along the cobbled thoroughfares.

Did anyone write the great 9/11 novel? I don't know. Maybe we all tried, even if we never intentionally set out to do so, and maybe we couldn't stop ourselves if we tried. What will the great writing about 2020 be like? An updated *Decameron*? An allegory like *The Plague*? A love story? A *Love in the Time of Cholera*? Will it be a war tale? A *Things They Carried*? What are the things we carried when we locked down, besides toilet paper and hand sanitizer? But what are we battling here in 2020, and who is at the front lines, besides all of us? Does the pandemic call us to conflict or to love, or is it both? Why would love be conflict-free or genuine conflict be devoid of love? Or will that plague story be told off to the side, a la *King Lear*, which was staged in the aftermath of a bubonic plague event that shuttered London theaters.

In the Simpson Literary Project, we have a glimmering as to where we have been and why we will still keep going. Since we cannot know anything for sure, we're resolving to make mistakes, but the good kind. (The esteemed epistemologist and philosopher catcher Yogi Berra on why his team lost a game: "We made too many of the wrong mistakes.") So okay, the right mistakes. But remember what Beckett wrote: "*Ever tried. Ever failed. No matter. Try again. Fail again. Fail better.*" We're going to never stop asking the hard questions. Because one thing that is happening all over the place is that people are facing up, in public view, to questions about their vulnerability to this virus, in other words, to their mortality. And that applies across the spectrum—to the mortality of ourselves, of our families, of our country, of our organizations and institutions, of our received ideas about all of them. So you better have a good answer as to why you're alive now. What do we have to live for? For starters, for our loved ones and everyone else's loved ones. For our values and principles. For art. As e.e. cummings said, "Always a more beautiful answer to a more beautiful question."

Here we are, the Simpson Literary Project, a little nonprofit with outsize plans, dreams, and objectives. These pandemics are hitting us—hitting our communities—hard with outsize consequences. We are not giving up. We have a story to tell, and it's your story, and our story. Storytellers forge a literate, democratic society, and that's a truth worth the struggle. Because storytellers and teachers are essential personnel, too.

~

Defoe concludes *A Journal of the Plague Year* with his bleak reflections about the "unthankfulness" and "wickedness" he supposedly witnessed. It is hard to fault him. Our own plague, our pandemic, brings out the best in some—as with our health care and essential workers, risking their lives, and our learned and dedicated epidemiologists and researchers.

And they bring out the worst as well—as with politicians absolutely beholden to a science-denying malignant narcissist of a president.

Defoe's narrator posed as an eyewitness, as we have all been eyewitnesses, and with these words, he reaches his end:

> *I can go no farther here. I should be counted censorious, and perhaps unjust, if I should enter into the unpleasing work of reflecting, whatever cause there was for it, upon the unthankfulness and return of all manner of wickedness among us, which I was so much an eye-witness of myself. I should conclude the account of this calamitous year with a coarse but sincere stanza of my own, which I placed at the end of my ordinary memorandums the same year they were written:*
>
> > *A dreadful plague in London was*
> > *In the year sixty-five,*
> > *Which swept an hundred thousand souls*
> > *Away; yet I alive.*

Someday, who knows when, let us hope we affirm that when this pandemic is done with us, and done with our loved ones, and done with our very democracy, and after it has annihilated so many—yet we (perhaps most of us) somehow survived. At what cost to our society, at what cost to our ravaged planet and to our battered communities and to all the hundreds of thousands of families who lost loved ones, we dread to contemplate. No wonder this is, in the words of Toni Morrison quoted earlier, "precisely the time when artists go to work."

And that's where the Simpson Literary Project comes in.

WORKS & DAYS

For an exhaustive yet nuanced catalogue of the national plague year, see *Unprepared: America in the Time of Coronavirus*, introduction by Timothy Egan, compiled and edited by Jon Sternfeld (Bloomsbury). This is a headshaking, stomach-churning, scrupulous record of this tormented period, December 2019-June 2020. So in that spirit, let me recollect below a few things that acutely affected the Project during our own plague year. What follows here is our *Works & Days*, to invoke the ancient Greek poet Hesiod's title. It purports to be a bare bones account of what happened, globally and nationally and locally, and how we were affected, believably unbelievable as it all may indeed be.

October 2019 (that is, Eons Ago)

October 12: Simpson Literary Project Annual Celebration at the Lafayette Library and Learning Center, Lafayette, CA; featuring 2019 Joyce Carol Oates Prize Winner Laila Lalami, students from Simpson Workshops at Girls Inc.-Alameda County and Northgate High School (Juvenile Hall incarcerated writers not permitted to attend), Moroccan music combo, and a dazzling Moroccan feast created and served by Peter Chastain & Prima Ristorante. (I hope this doesn't come off in the wrong way, and that this isn't misinterpreted, but the truth is nobody throws a better party than the SLP, nobody.)

PGE "planned" power outages threatened the event; plans were being made up until the last minute to stage it elsewhere—at my house if necessary. Finally, power flipped on, and we went forward. I can report there was, in several senses, *electricity* in the air.

2020 Joyce Carol Oates Prize Longlist announced.

November 2019

Laila Lalami, 2019 Joyce Carol Oates Prize Winner, is named finalist for the National Book Award in Fiction, for her novel *The Other Americans*.

December 2019

The impeachment of Donald Trump, the forty-fifth president of the United States, was initiated on 18 December 2019, when the House of Representatives approved articles of impeachment on charges of abuse of power and obstruction of Congress. The Senate acquitted Trump of these charges on 5 February 2020.

December 31: Closing stock market numbers:
DJIA—28,538.44
S&P—3,230.78
NASDAQ—8,945.99

The national unemployment rate at the end of 2019 was 3.5%; it would rise to a high of 14.7% in April 2020.

January 2020

First confirmed case of COVID-19 in the United States.

Jury at work establishing the shortlist of finalists for the 2020 Joyce Carol Oates Prize.

January 22:
TRUMP: It's one person coming in from China, and we have it under control. It's going to be just fine. [He will say something along these lines twenty-two times in the coming months.]

February 2020

February 6: First recorded death in the United States—a woman in California—attributed to novel virus COVID-19.

Italy, China, and elsewhere hammered by the virus. In Italy, especially the North, carabieneri posted on street corners to stop people from wandering from home without a specific, limited purpose (like shopping for food or going to the farmacia).

SLP renames our prize the Joyce Carol Oates (JCO) Prize.

Shortlisted Finalists for 2020 JCO Prize announced:

Chris Bachelder, Maria Dahvana Headley, Rebecca Makkai, Daniel Mason, Peter Orner, Dexter Palmer, Kevin Wilson. A murderer's row of mid-career authors of fiction.

The President of the United States: "The virus, it's like a miracle, is just going to go away."

February 26:
TRUMP: When you have 15 people. And the 15 within a couple of days is going to be down to close to zero, that's a pretty good job we've done.

March 2020

After extensive preparation, the Board of SLP engages in systematic, long-range, strategic planning exercises. File under cruel irony: Yes, planning, great idea, then comes the pandemic. *I got your plan right here,* says the virus.

~~JCO's planned trip to the Bay Area: cancelled.~~

~~JCO & Laila Lalami, headlining SLP fundraising event at Sharon Simpson's home: cancelled.~~

~~JCO & Laila Lalami in conversation with Joe Di Prisco at the sold-out Lafayette Library: cancelled.~~

~~Laila Lalami 10-day residency at the University of California, Berkeley, and in Lafayette: cancelled.~~

~~SLP Annual Dinner at Prima Ristorante: cancelled.~~

~~The four SLP writing workshops postponed indefinitely or cancelled.~~

~~SLP programming fundraising for the year grinds to a halt.~~

Country partially shuts down, state by state, chaotically, without a national plan. There will never be a national plan to respond to the pandemic as long as Trump is president.

New York: virus is out of control.

Lockdowns in California and elsewhere.

Schools close.

Stores close.

Book orders soar—people need to read. Meanwhile publishers' accounts receivable grievously suffer, as bookstores—including Amazon's—slow-pay their accounts payable. Amazon, slow-paying. Let me be clear: Amafreakingzon slow-pays and deems books "nonessential" services.

Food delivery becomes commonplace.

Gloves and masks become a thing.

Toilet paper and cleaning products become like gold, vanishing from shelves real and online.

Alcohol and drug consumption booming.

Restaurants and bars close, disproportionately affecting the lives of writers everywhere. (But this is not being glib, not in the slightest.)

Netflix Hulu Amazon/Prime Peacock Disney Streaming Streaming Streaming...

(Who knew there were so many lousy shows to binge-un-watch? Maybe it's just that there are too many good choices, or not enough good choices, or maybe that Netflix has yet to option one of my books, but I digress. On the other hand, watch the magnificent *My Octopus Teacher*, the not-great title of a beautiful, moving documentary about—an octopus, and everything else that matters.)

March 9, a.k.a. Black Monday: Many consider the 2020 crash to have started on this day, with the Dow falling 2,013 points, the worst single-day point drop in US market history, to 23,851.02 (7.79%).

March 23: The lowest closing values this year were on this day:
 DJIA—18,591.93, down 34.85% since 12/31
 S&P—2,237.40, down 30.75% since 12/31
 NASDAQ—6,860.67, down 23.31% since 12/31

March 20: California issues stay-at-home orders.

March 28: 2020 JCO Prize finalist Daniel Mason publishes an op-ed in *The New York Times,* "How a College Final Became a Lesson in Survival."

"Back in January, at Stanford University, where I teach and practice psychiatry, I showed my students a slide of an oak tree from the edge of campus.

"At first the photo seemed out of place. The course, 'PSYC82: The Literature of Psychosis,' is about the portrayal of psychosis in memoir and fiction, art and film; the lecture that day was a survey of psychiatric history. But there is growing evidence linking green space to mental well-being, and I have become increasingly concerned for my students, who, studies show, are experiencing depression and anxiety at record rates. I wanted them to get outside. The winter had been mild, a new round of rains had just passed through, and the woods were beautiful."

As the pandemic disrupts life at college, and as students returned to their homes around the country, he conceives an inspired assignment. He asks them, from wherever they may be, to "Go outside and take a photo of the natural world we had talked about so often, and share it with others in the class." The results surprised and moved him and everyone in the class. "Over the next few days, the photos continued to flow in, nearly 100, from the Central Valley, Hawaii and Indonesia. There were familiar campus ginkgoes, cedars in Brooklyn, polypore mushrooms climbing a tree in Utah. The assignment was called—because on the spur of the moment I couldn't think of anything else—'The World Around Us.' And that was what the students had built."

"It is worth remembering, as this story unfolds, that we are being sustained not only by the neighbors who bring groceries, and the teachers who learn how to manage a classroom of rowdy kindergartners on Zoom, and the doctors and nurses and hospital staff who are risking their lives for a country that can't, or won't, supply them with enough protective equipment, but also by the oaks and fritillaries, the gardens and copses of cottonwoods that are so critical to both our physical and mental well-being."

The President of the United States: "The virus, it's like a miracle, is just going to go away."

Deaths and infections in the United States rise precipitously. We are not flattening the curve.

April 2020

Dr. Anthony Fauci becomes the solitary, reasoned voice of sanity and humanity; his elevation to hero seems like a foregone conclusion, even as his job status seems more tenuous by the day, because, obviously, Trump.

Simpson Writing Workshop at McKinley High School, Contra Costa Juvenile Hall: cancelled.

Simpson Writing Workshop at Girls Inc.-Alameda County: two workshops conducted virtually.

Simpson Writing Workshop at Northgate High School: proceeds improvisationally, occasionally.

Virus spreads how? Really, nobody knows. Aerosolized droplets? Contact contamination? How come nobody knows for sure? And yet, that's epidemiology at work, thankfully, painstakingly.

With people not driving and with industry on hiatus, air quality is better than ever.

In Venice, Italy, dolphins are sighted in the canals for the first time in ages.

Trump on TV every day for hours and hours.

April 23. The Madness of King Trump Unabated: He suggests injecting disinfectant bleach to beat the virus and clean the lungs.

Not to mention: The Madness of Trump's Hydroxycloroquine Delusion. "What do you have to lose?" Doctors quickly answered: Your lives. (People with lupus, who need the lifesaving drug, which is contraindicated to treat COVID-19, freak out, as supplies for them are put at risk.)

SLP postpones awarding the 2020 JCO prize.

SLP reflects on how now to serve our communities of readers and writers of all generations.

SLP staff and contractors volunteer to work at 80 percent compensation. Two workshops at Girls Inc. in Downtown Oakland work beautifully through Zoom. Northgate High School has some success, too. Contra Costa Juvenile Hall is unable to host the two scheduled workshops.

Sarah Cooper becomes a star we never could have imagined we needed so badly: A brilliant Black comedian mockingly lip-synching Trump's words somehow makes him seem both sublimely ridiculous and all too threatening.

The President of the United States: "The virus, it's like a miracle, is just going to go away."

May 2020

YES, A MASK, OF COURSE, A PRUDENT, SIMPLE, LIFE-SAVING IDEA

May 8: "The American economy plunged deeper into crisis last month, losing 20.5 million jobs as the unemployment rate jumped to 14.7 percent, the worst devastation since the Great Depression. The Labor Department's monthly report on Friday provided the clearest picture yet of the breadth and depth of the economic damage—and how swiftly it spread—as the coronavirus pandemic swept the country." *The New York Times*

May 12: Daniel Mason is named 2020 Joyce Carol Oates Prize Recipient. The SLP Board of Directors selected Daniel from a most distinguished shortlist of finalists. The award-winning author of *The Winter Soldier* (Little, Brown), he is Clinical Assistant Professor in the Stanford University Department of Psychiatry, and author of four influential, powerful books of fiction, including the just published *A Registry of My Passage Upon the Earth* (Little, Brown). He will appear, it is hoped, in the Bay Area in October 2020 and participate in ten-day residency during the spring semester of 2021. He is the fourth winner of the annual $50,000 award.

[So said the press release, back when we had no idea what the year would be like.]

"The Winter Soldier is a deeply moving, imaginatively audacious achievement: the evoking of a bygone world with such precision, such richness of detail and empathy, the reader is reminded of those scenes in Tolstoy's War and Peace *that bring us into the very narrative, as if we were, not readers peering back into an historic past, but contemporaries of that past caught up in its heartrending drama. Those with a particular interest in the history of medical science will be fascinated by Daniel Mason's young doctor's medical adventures in the most primitive of settings—the battlefield."*

—Joyce Carol Oates

May 24: Front page Sunday banner headline in *The New York Times*:

U.S. DEATHS NEAR 100,000, AN INCALCULABLE LOSS

The names of one thousand casualties take up the entire front page, continuing inside.

May 25: Amy Cooper calls cops on a birdwatcher in Central Park, Christian Cooper, after he politely asks her to leash her dog. She tells police that "an African American man is threatening my life." News spreads instantly. She is castigated as the archetypal "Karen," and loses her job after she apologizes. (How many babies born in the foreseeable future will be named Karen?) The district attorney signals that the office will pursue her for filing a false report. Mr. Cooper (no relation to his accuser) thinks she has suffered enough and elects not to assist in prosecution.

"I CAN'T BREATHE."

May 25: George Floyd is murdered, his casual execution caught on camera, by four policemen in Minneapolis, a knee to his neck for eight minutes and forty-six seconds, as he said over and over again that he could not breathe, his last words a plea for his dead mother.

The nation erupts, in overwhelmingly peaceful protests.

Yes, there are criminals and idiots and anarchists, of course, who take advantage of the chaos, but still: overwhelmingly peaceful protests across the nation.

May 31: "A Decade of Watching Black People Die," NPR.

Eric Garner had just broken up a fight, according to witness testimony.

Ezell Ford was walking in his neighborhood.

Michelle Cusseaux was changing the lock on her home's door when police arrived to take her to a mental health facility.

Tanisha Anderson was having a bad mental health episode, and her brother called 911.

Tamir Rice was playing in a park.

Natasha McKenna was having a schizophrenic episode when she was tazed in Fairfax, Va.

Walter Scott was going to an auto-parts store.

Bettie Jones answered the door to let Chicago police officers in to help her upstairs neighbor, who had called 911 to resolve a domestic dispute.

Philando Castile was driving home from dinner with his girlfriend.

Botham Jean was eating ice cream in his living room in Dallas.

Atatiana Jefferson was babysitting her nephew at home in Fort Worth, Texas.

Eric Reason was pulling into a parking spot at a local chicken and fish shop.

Dominique Clayton was sleeping in her bed.

Breonna Taylor was also asleep in her bed.

And George Floyd was at the grocery store.

Etc., etc., etc.

Some police and politicians and other leaders take a knee during demonstrations in support of reform.

The body politic begins the painful process of considering next steps in the administration of criminal justice and the exercise of police community resources.

Every rational person grasps the connection between social unrest and viral contagion and income inequality.

Social unrest. Mass BLM marches in NYC, LA, Portland, Chicago, Seattle, the Bay Area, many other localities. *Defund the Police* becomes a rallying cry, while some activists committed to the cause prefer *Reform the Police*, believing that *Defund* is a gift to the Right, and some Black leaders cry out that we need to add to the budget of law enforcement, all the while rethinking what that means, especially for people of color. Past time for criminal justice reform.

The President of the United States: "The virus, it's like a miracle, is just going to go away."

June 2020

PUT ON A DAMN MASK.

June 1: Trump orders the military to tear-gas BLM protestors in Lafayette Square Park, in order to create a photo-op before a church while toting the Bible.

Parts of the nation foolishly, precipitously reopen to cater to the whims and craven political designs of the President. Infections soar, post-Memorial Day.

Polls show unprecedented broad and deep support of anti-racism, along with support for widespread police reform.

The NFL says it was mistaken with regard to Colin Kaepernick and the whole kneeling down thing. Mistaken? They meant to say gutless and racist.

SLP formally granted by the IRS 501(c)3 nonprofit status. We have always been from the start a nonprofit, thanks to our fortunate association with the Lafayette Library and Learning Center Foundation, our original fiscal sponsor. We will begin to transition in due course, as we try our new wings.

Antiracism books fly off the shelves. Yes, great news, critics are remarking, but will people do the hard work of enacting antiracism? One thing to read a book and internalize. Another thing, to act. Some observers decry whites' book-buying as being "performative."

Vaccines in development, it seems, though many question and doubt. Some days there are auspicious reports. But as many said, "Vaccines, yes, are important. But what's more important is vaccinations. That is, will there be enough of them available to be distributed and will enough of the herd-immunity fools take them? And what to do with all the anti-vaxxers and COVID-19-deniers?"

The federal administration decides to throw its weight behind preserving Confederate monuments. Let's try that again. Trump decides to champion protecting Confederate monuments.

June 26: "You Want a Confederate Monument? My Body is a Confederate Monument," by the poet Caroline Randall Williams. This commanding op-ed blows up on the pages of *The New York Times*, and it should forever be a last word on this subject, I hope:

NASHVILLE — *"I have rape-colored skin. My light-brown-blackness is a living testament to the rules, the practices, the causes of the Old South.*

"If there are those who want to remember the legacy of the Confederacy, if they want monuments, well, then, my body is a monument. My skin is a monument."

Forty million people out of work in the US.

The President of the United States: "The virus, it's like a miracle, is just going to go away."

July 2020

PUT ON YOUR FUCKING MASK.

July 1:

Trump: "I think we're gonna be very good with the coronavirus. I think that at some point that's going to sort of just disappear. I hope. I'll be right eventually. I will be right eventually. You know I said, 'It's going to disappear.' I'll say it again."

Strangest Fourth of July in modern memory. What are we celebrating? Is our democracy under siege?

COVID-19 spikes throughout the land.

Major League Baseball and the National Basketball Association hatch seemingly harebrained schemes to play ball—and they look shakier by the day, though the NBA may have a shot to succeed because players will stay in a "bubble." The National Football League and The National Hockey Association—what is going to happen there?

The magnificent Prima Ristorante, in Walnut Creek, CA, led by chef/owner and dear friend Peter Chastain, cherished SLP home for celebrations, regretfully announces it is closing permanently. This feels very much like a death in our family.

July 7:

Hi Mr. Wood [David Wood, high school teacher and SLP board member],
    I know this message is a bit late, but I just wanted to say a huge thank you for everything that you did to promote writing and bring out the

goodness of the students you knew, including myself. I'm forever grateful for the work you did to facilitate and execute an amazing creative writing club. Word out on the street says you're also a pretty great teacher, too.

I despise the fact that the in-person school year ended long before it normally would have, and that creative writing was directly affected as a result. Most of all, I'm disappointed that there was never a real opportunity to say a true goodbye.

Despite this, some of my fondest memories during my four years at Northgate are from Wednesdays, after school, in room 33. That's when we had our own little community of talented writers, and it felt very different from the rest of high school in the best way possible. It's something I was, and will always be, proud to be a part of.

I hope you've been managing well these last few months. I've been doing a little writing, reading and volunteering, nothing too crazy. I'll be attending UC Davis this fall, where I'll be double majoring in Urban Planning and Political Science. Since I've decided to live at home for at least the first half of the upcoming school year, I'll be able to visit Northgate, if visitors are permitted. Rest assured, I'll certainly pay a visit to room 33.

Best wishes,

Jackson

Teenagers' coronavirus parties become a thing, prompting learned analysis of the prefrontal cortex in adolescent development along with gobsmacked disbelief on the part of former teenagers everywhere.

July 10: Trump commutes the sentence of Roger Stone, convicted of, among other charges, lying in order to protect the president. The unprecedented corruption excoriated by perennially-late-to-the-party Senator Mitt Romney:

"*Unprecedented, historic corruption: An American president commutes the sentence of a person convicted by a jury of lying to shield that very president.*"

July 11: 792 people died today in the US of Covid-19

July 11: Trump puts on a mask in public the first time, wears it (inadvisably, uselessly) below the nose, visiting Walter Reed Medical Center (Walter Reed, infectious disease Hall of Famer). What is the latest estimate of fatalities and infections that would have been avoided with the adoption of masking by 90 percent?

United States	Confirmed	Recovered	Deaths
	3.37M	989K	137K
Worldwide	Confirmed	Recovered	Deaths
	12.9M	7M	571K

July 17: John Lewis, Civil Rights leader and more than a secular saint, dies, age eighty.

July 20: Now Trump seems to say that wearing a mask is "patriotic," even as he muddles and qualifies the issue by tweeting that "many people are saying it is Patriotic to wear a mask." ("Many people are saying...": his tag line preface for disinformation and deceit.)

July 31: Banner headline, front page, *The New York Times*:

VIRUS WIPES OUT 5 YEARS OF ECONOMIC GROWTH

The President of the United States: "The virus, it's like a miracle, is just going to go away."

136,000 deaths in the US.

August 2020

IT WON'T KILL YOU TO PUT ON A FUCKING MASK.

August 3: In response to a reporter's question about the 150,000+ deaths in America, Trump says: "It is what it is."

August 3: In the United States, one death due to COVID-19 every minute.

August 4: *"We are in a nightmare, and have been for a long time. But nightmares, like pandemics, eventually end. The most important question to keep in front of us, in the long night of the coming months, is who will we be when we wake?"*—Terence Holt, "With Pandemic Information Overload How Can We Tell What is Real?" (*Lithub*)

August 4: The Governor of California: "Tournaments, events, or competitions, regardless of whether teams are from the same school or from different schools, counties, or states are not permitted at this time."

The President of the United States, with hand gestures of dismissal: "The virus is just going to go away."

Aug 3: Deaths and infections US/World: rising and rising and rising.

United States	Confirmed	Recovered	Deaths
	4.78M	2.32M	158K
Worldwide	Confirmed	Recovered	Deaths
	18.1M	10.8M	691K

September 2020

FIRES FIRES FIRES

WHERE'S YOUR STUPID MASK?

Bob Woodward's *Rage* is released, in which Trump is quoted as he was taped, speaking on the record, about the virus. He knew the virus was for real in February, that it was more dangerous than the flu, and that people could contract the disease via the air. He then went out all winter and spring saying it was nothing, it would go away, like a miracle. He said he didn't want people to panic.

Laila Lalami publishes a trenchant work of nonfiction, *Conditional Citizens: On Belonging in America*. Lalami poignantly illustrates how white supremacy survives through adaptation and legislation, with the result that a caste system is maintained that keeps the modern equivalent of white male landowners at the top of the social hierarchy. Conditional citizens, she argues, are all the people with whom America embraces with one arm and pushes away with the other.

Will schools open? Will colleges and universities? How many educational institutions will fail to survive? Will high school, collegiate, and professional sports take place? Will we ever go to a restaurant or church or concert or play again?

September 19: Supreme Court Justice Ruth Bader Ginzburg dies.

September 20: Equinox for SLP at the California Shakespeare Theater: A safely distanced gathering of fifty friends of the SLP in the 500-seat outdoor theater. A beautiful evening.

Michael Krasny, author, professor, and beloved public radio host and interviewer, is awarded the SLP inaugural Simpsonista Award in recognition of his lifelong dedication to readers and writers.

October 2020

PUT ON YOUR FUCKING MASK.

October 2: "For New Yorkers, the prospect of seeing the normally brilliant west side of Lincoln Center darkened for another year—as the Metropolitan Opera announced last week that it has canceled its entire 2020-21 season—is heartbreaking. For the rest of the country, though, it should be equally alarming. If even the Met, one of the nation's premier cultural institutions, can't come back, is covid-19 now pushing America's performing arts past the point of no return?...

"Ninety percent of the member organizations of the National Independent Venue Association polled in a recent survey warned that, without government aid, they will close permanently in a few months. The disastrous impact would ripple across the economy: Before the coronavirus struck, the performing arts and their associated industries collectively employed some five million Americans and accounted for $900 billion in economic activity—4.5 percent of the gross domestic product." *The Washington Post*

Oct 2: There were more than 301,000 new Covid-19 cases in the US in the past week, according to the US Centers for Disease Control and Prevention. One of the new cases is the President of the United States, Donald J. Trump, who is helicoptered to Walter Reed Hospital, where a team of doctors treats him with remedies unavailable to the general public.

Earlier on Friday, before Trump went into hospital, [Chris] Wallace appeared on Fox & Friends and told viewers: "Wear the damn mask."

"Follow the science," he said.

"If I could say one thing to all of the people out there watching: Forget the politics. This is a public safety health issue."

Oct 4: *USA Today*: There were more than 54,000 positive cases of the coronavirus reported on Friday, the highest single-day case count since Aug. 14, when the country recorded just over 64,000 cases, per Johns Hopkins University data.

More than 209,000 Americans dead of COVID-19.

This is the moment when our very own Aristophanes, Sophocles, Mark Twain, Dorothy Parker, Oscar Wilde, and Charles Dickens should take their cues and step up to illuminate the darkness of our times. But the next person who references Trump's illness by invoking the term "irony" should be punched (distantly) in the news—I mean *nose*.

Oct 5: "[T]he president added a piece of advice in his announcement of his hospital discharge: "Don't be afraid of Covid. Don't let it dominate your life."

"If only the 209,000 Americans who have died of this disease without immediate access to the drugs and facilities the president benefited from had been able to be less afraid. I am sure that would have solved it. As sure as I am of anything, now."

Alexandra Petri, *The Washington Post*

Oct 19: The Simpson Literary Project shoots *Shakespeare & the Plague*, the movie.

Deaths and infections overtax hospitals in US and the rest of the world.

Oct 22: "The U.S. recorded 71,671 new coronavirus cases on Thursday, the most in one day since the outbreak hit alarming heights in July, according to data compiled by Johns Hopkins University . One day earlier, around 63,000 new cases had been reported. The U.S. also recorded 856 deaths from COVID-19 on Thursday, raising the death toll to more than 223,000 people lost to the pandemic." *The Wall Street Journal*

Oct 23: "The country reported more than 83,700 new Covid-19 cases on Friday, passing the last record of roughly 77,300 cases seen on July 16 as the U.S. grappled with outbreaks in Sun Belt states, according to data compiled by Johns Hopkins University." *CNBC*

November 2020

WHAT'S WRONG WITH YOU? KEEP YOUR MASK ON SO OTHER PEOPLE AND YOU YOURSELF DON'T DIE.

2021 JCO Prize Longlist established.

SLP short film released nationwide, available for free viewing, serving students and teachers, with the hope that it goes, well, viral:

The Simpson Literary Project presents Shakespeare & the Plague. *Shakespeare lived his entire life in the shadow of a plague, and his plays reference dread and disruption familiar to us during our own pandemic. Pulitzer Prize-winner Stephen Greenblatt of Harvard University, General Editor of The Norton Shakespeare, introduces this mash-up curated by Philippa Kelly and performed by the Pandemic Popup Players.*

Filmed by Obatala Mawusi and Fox Nakai at the California Shakespeare Theater. Music by Paul Dresher. Directed by Philippa Kelly. Produced by Joseph Di Prisco.

Nov 3: The United States Presidential election, the epitome of consequentiality: Joe Biden vs. Donald Trump. Trump barnstorms through swing states, leading rallies attended by the idiotic maskless. Biden is eventually declared winner, amassing over 81,000,000 votes, 7,000,000 more than Trump, who does not and may never concede, electing instead to file frivolous lawsuits and spread disinformation about supposed fraud in the election, thereby spreading doubt about the very nature of the constitutional democracy, and musing about declaring martial law. In other words, Trump and cohorts attempt to disenfranchise voters and steal the election. The term for that is coup. The courts, however, continually reject all his many, manic, illiterate lawsuits. It was the freest, fairest election of all time in the United States.

Nov 17: 11,000,000 Americans infected

100,000-170,000 new cases each day for the last two weeks in the United States

250,000+ Americans dead of the virus

"On Friday, more than 195,500 new infections were reported—the country's highest for a single day, and far beyond what the nation was seeing just weeks ago. The highest number of single-day cases during the country's summer surge was a little more than 77,100 in July, Johns Hopkins University data show. The US on Friday also recorded its highest number of Covid-19 patients in hospitals on a given day: 82,178." COVID TRACKING PROJECT

Nov 21: "I want to hit the button that says, 'Resume life.' But this is life now and we shouldn't waste it," op-ed by Stephen Petrow in *The Washington Post*:

"I thought again about my friend's question, 'How do you think we'll adjust to life when it starts up again?' Here's my answer: Life has not stopped. But we may need to move more slowly, with greater awareness of each moment. Maybe start with just changing how we do the dishes."

US coronavirus deaths (weekdays): Nov 2: 567; Nov 3: 1,004; Nov 4: 1,571; Nov 5: 1,369; Nov 6: 1,185–Nov 9: 789; Nov 10: 1,305; Nov 11: 1,534; Nov 12: 1,136; Nov 13: 1,270–Nov 16: 894; Nov 17: 1,527; Nov 18: 1,798; Nov 19: 1,945; Nov 20: 1,904–Nov 23: 1,164

Nov. 25: "A growing number of Americans are going hungry. 26 million now say they don't have enough to eat, as the pandemic worsens and the holidays near." *The Washington Post*

According to Johns Hopkins University, more than 261,000 people have died from Covid-19 in the United States. More than 12.7 million people have been diagnosed with the virus and the United States has set several new daily records for hospitalizations.

Thanksgiving travel and get-togethers threaten to become the mother of superspreading events.

US Coronavirus cases:
    Apr 28—1 Million
    Jun 10—2 Million
    Jul 7—3 Million
    Jul 23—4 Million
    Aug 8—5 Million
    Aug 30—6 Million

Sept 24—7 Million
Oct 15—8 Million
Oct 29—9 Million
Nov 8—10 Million
Nov 15—11 Million
Nov 21—12 Million
Nov 27—13 Million

2021

Simpsonistas: Tales from the Simpson Literary Project Vol. 3 published.

Vaccinations underway across the country and the world.

When will the pandemic be over, if ever?

Do we dare to hope?

Finally, humble thanks to so many of you who have generously supported—financially, morally, emotionally, spiritually—the Project. All our writers, readers, and students are indebted to you.

Joseph Di Prisco, Editor

Founding Chair, Simpson Literary Project

jdp@simpsonliteraryproject.org

DANIEL MASON
2020 JOYCE CAROL OATES PRIZE RECIPIENT

THE WINTER SOLDIER

AN EXCERPT

Dusk was falling when they came over a low hill and at last found themselves before a village. It was tucked in a softly sloping valley, with two streets of houses descending from a single wooden church of rough-hewn logs. Above the church, the road kept rising. Below, the valley widened into snow-covered fields that flanked a frozen river. "Lemnowice," said the hussar. They followed the road down to the fields and then up past the houses. They were low-ceilinged huts, made of wood, straw-thatched, with tiny windows, all covered with wooden shutters so that it was impossible to see inside. There were no chimneys. A pair of drays lay in the road, seemingly abandoned, half-buried in snow. There was a flutter over one of the rooftops, and a huge black crow took off into the sky.

There was not a soul in sight. He saw no garrison, no sign of the army at all, certainly nothing that could be a hospital. Perhaps it lay beyond the hill, he thought. Unless this, too, had been a mistake. If, after such a journey, he would have to turn around.

The hussar stopped before the church, motioning Lucius to descend. He obeyed, approached the door, and knocked. He waited. There was a narrow window in the door that reminded him of an arrow slit in a castle. The hussar told him to knock harder, and only then did he hear movement, the sound of footsteps. In the window, an eye appeared.

"Krzelewski," said Lucius. "Medical lieutenant. Fourteenth Regiment, Third Army."

Then a key in the lock, the clang of the mechanism. The door opened to reveal a nursing sister. She wore a stiff grey habit, and from her hand dangled a Mannlicher rifle, standard issue of the *K.u.K.*

"May I speak to the supervising physician?" he asked in German.

When she didn't answer, he tried Polish.

"The doctor?" she replied, still staying back, in the shadows. "Didn't you just say you're him?"

~

The nurse's name was Margarete. She gave no surname. It was not the custom of the Sisters of St. Catherine to do so, she would explain. Even Margarete was a name she had assumed with her vows, abandoning her earthly appellation from the life she led before. Her face floated in the darkness of the narthex, and it was only when Lucius turned to see the hussar kick his horse and ride away (*flee*, thought Lucius later) that she opened the door more widely, motioning for him to step inside with a sweeping of the gun. Then she threw her shoulder against the door. He stood in total darkness while she secured it, first turning the iron lock, then heaving a crossbar into the cleats. Turning to follow her movement, he heard a key slip into a second door, then the sonorous clanging of the mechanism as it engaged. Then, weapon swinging in her hand, she led him into the dim light of the nave.

As Lucius's habit upon entering a house of God was to look up at the majesty of the ceiling, his first impression was that the church of Lemnowice was much like any other of the dozens of wooden churches he had visited in the Tatras, further west, though this, with its heavy dome and tiny windows, suggested more an Eastern rite. A row of six wooden columns supported the ceiling, from which a pair of chains dangled, now empty of their chandeliers. In the distance, the north transept was illuminated by a lantern. The rest of the church was dark.

It was the sounds and smell that made him look down. A low moan from somewhere in the darkness. A cough, a laboured breath. An acrid odour, something animal, like spoiled meat. He looked. The pews were gone, and in their place were lumps of blankets, and it was only when he saw one stir that he understood they were men.

Three rows, perhaps fifteen or twenty lumps in each.

By then Sister Margarete had finished locking the second door and appeared at his side. Softly, she said, "If I may speak?"

Lucius nodded, unable to take his eyes off the bodies.

"The doctor, Szökefalvi, a Hungarian," she said, "Szökefalvi, your predecessor, vanished two months ago under circumstances which perhaps Pan Doctor Lieutenant should understand."

Now Lucius turned, struck by her form of address, a combination of Polish honorific and German military rank. For a moment, he studied her. She was more than a head shorter than him, and her face was framed by the impeccably crisp folds of her wimple, which pressed in upon her cheeks. Her eyes were of indistinct colour, glassy, her lips parted with the impatience of one who wished to speak. He guessed she was a year or two older than he was. The giant key hung like a cross from a chain around her neck, and she had yet to set down her gun.

Again, she seemed to await his blessing. "Yes, please, go on," he said. Then, quietly, drawing him aside, so that she could speak without being heard by the soldiers on the floor before them, she began.

"In the beginning there were seven of us, Pan Doctor Lieutenant: myself and Sisters Maria and Libuše and Elizabeth and Klara, and two doctors—one whose name deserves no utterance and Szökefalvi, poor Szökefalvi, whom I've come to forgive. We were but a simple casualty clearing station then. Patch up and send along, as they say. It wasn't until September that the High Command appreciated our sheltered position in the valley and upgraded us to the status of a Regimental Hospital, receiving the wounded from the battlefield and caring for them until they were ready to be evacuated to the rear. We had an X-ray machine and a bacteriology laboratory, and with daily prayer and sharp knives and carbolic acid for antisepsis of the wound, we performed a great service for the brave young men serving this smaller, terrestrial king. For three months, we attended to them: castigations of mine and sword, of howitzer, ecrasite and poisonous earth. We resurrected men shot through with every bullet in the devil's armoury, men struck by high explosive and Cossack swords, men who lost their feet and hands to the winter when they fell asleep. Such was our glory, Pan Doctor, it brings tears of joy to my eyes to contemplate it once again. Even when the X-ray machine was taken off to Tarnów, and our last drop of eosin had illuminated the mysteries of the last bacteriologic slide—even then we prevailed. For two more months we prevailed. But with so many prayers rising to heaven, Doctor, not only here in Galicia, but from the Pripet, and from the

Bukovina and Bessarabia, and—now I have heard—far and beyond, from the cities of Flanders and Friuli, Serbia, Macedonia, and from the great city of Warsaw—yes, with so many lips turned toward our Lord's ever attentive ears, and His angels labouring without rest, deflecting bullets with their angelic breath and giving heat to frozen bodies in the snow—with so many lips turned to heaven, one could not expect His eternal protection for ever. So we forgave Him and took no affront when the fortress of Przemyśl was seized, and He sent His angels on to that city and left us to the mercy of the Louse."

She paused. For the last word, she had spoken in German—*Laus*—and with it her face contorted briefly in disgust.

"You are familiar with the Louse, Doctor. I had known Her too well as a child, and indeed from the very first days of the war She was with us. But never have I known Her in such abundance as in this house of prayer. As the war drew on, we found ourselves confronted with ever greater infestations. Never, never, dear Doctor, have I seen such extraordinary fertility in any beast; indeed, in my moments of least faith I have wondered if it was the Louse that is God's favoured child. For it seemed at times that one could subtract all matter from our worldly domain but the Louse, and still Earth's contours could be seen. Oh, Doctor, as a child I had imagined the animals of Noah to be tame, clean creatures, with soft, sweet-smelling hair and soft noses to caress. No! Now I realize that they all must have been infested, not only the rat, but the lion and weasel, the vicious giraffe: veritable arks themselves, for worm and tick and louse.

"For you cannot imagine the infestations of our men. Everywhere! On every layer of clothing, in every stitch and seam. In churning clumps, they teemed, they stirred, like embers. They came out upon our combs, grainy, like wet meal. Oh, sir, the devil has had time to practise since poor Job! For if the Beast truly wished to try that man's faith, he would have given him a field dressing in Galicia. No, there is nothing that arouses a Louse like the moist, warm dressing of a wound, nothing that heightens their incest more. A dressing applied one week prior in Lemberg would be teeming with so many rutting creatures that one could hear the soft thumps of the clots as they fell to the floor."

She took a deep breath.

"Of course, the Louse might torture, but as I've learned, She doesn't kill alone. The first case of typhus appeared in December, Doctor. I still remember the boy, the warmth of his skin, the rash as it spread across his chest and limbs, the peculiar thoughts that entered his mind and made him cry out. Try as we may, we couldn't save him, and it was not long before a second soldier, there—" and she pointed to the far corner of the room— "and a third—there—and a fourth—there—came down with the disease. Night and day we worked to save them, but no amount of lime or cresol could clean them. No quarantine could stall their advance. And no matter how tight we made our clothing—" and her eyes traced the edges of her wimple— "it did not matter. In the evenings, when I inspected the skin of Libuše, and Libuše Elizabeth, and Elizabeth Klara, and Klara myself-we would find the creatures on our very own flesh.

"Oh! Such was the state of affairs, Pan Doctor Lieutenant, when fear of Her first entered the heart of the good Hungarian doctor Szökefalvi. Even now, I feel such love for Szökefalvi— with his books and his patient lessons in nursing, with his innocent jokes of how he might like to join in our hours of delousing. He did not succumb at first, brave soul! I know so well the terror that seized him as he stood at the operating table and felt Her upon him. I saw him fight to direct his thoughts back to the case beneath his hands. Yet once you feel Her, you can't escape; once the itching begins, you cannot stop it, no, Pan Doctor Lieutenant: the slightest hair, the slightest tickle of wool is enough to conjure armies crawling across your skin. Even now if I am not strong, I can imagine Her crawling upon my knee, rising, her little prickling legs, her probing tongue. No! Oh, no, no, no! No, Pan Doctor Lieutenant Krzelewski: to survive, one must learn to fight such fantasies. But not so poor Szökefalvi. In the middle of surgery, gloves wet with gore, I would see him twitch. Not a great motion at first, I tell you, just a pause with the knife, but I knew that he had felt Her. That deep within his woollens She had begun to crawl. Up his leg or foot or belly, and he would start to cut again, and She would crawl, and he would stop, and start, and stop, and all of a sudden put down his knife and tear off his gloves, the once steady hands trembling as he tore at his clothes for the offending itch. At first this man respected rules of modesty, moving swiftly into the vestry to disrobe. But as the weeks passed, he became so panicked, so harried, that he forgot my very presence, baring those parts that shouldn't be seen." Her eyes bore into him. "Can you imagine the shock? I too feel Her crawling, Doctor, but I am of a nursing order, and if it is my fate to fall by Her bite, then it is so. I do not lose my dignity. St. Catherine ate the scabs of the afflicted, and so I remain strong before my wards. This is my duty. Looking at a crushed skull, I feel no fear. I do not falter before gangrene. No! I see not death before me, Doctor, I see the glimmer of my heavenly crown. I do not hear screams, but the chorus that will greet me. And when I feel the Louse upon me, I do not thrust my hands into my habit like some orang-utan of Portugal, but turn my thoughts to my Father on his throne. But Szökefalvi, Doctor, gripped by such fear, was not so strong. Nowhere was he safe. Even in the fields, on his walks, I saw him tearing at his clothes, stripping madly in the cold. At night, I heard him weeping, begging our pest to leave him alone. So often did he wash himself with cresol that his skin began to peel away, which made matters worse still, for then it was impossible to know whether it was the Louse or his own mortified flesh that tickled in his brain. Yet no words could get him to change."

She stopped. Now she seemed to be awaiting his response.

He said simply, "And this other doctor, Szökefalvi, he left?"

"In December." She lowered her voice. "If you will excuse your servant in venturing an opinion, I think he lost his mind. One morning I awoke and he was gone. But what do I know? You have studied in the great city of Vienna. Perhaps there you have heard of such a mad disease?"

But Lucius was looking over the vastness of the room. "And the other nurses?"

"The other nurses, Pan Doctor Lieutenant?"

"They fled, too?"

"Oh, no. Sister Maria died of typhus and Libuše died of typhus and Elizabeth of typhus, too. All save Sister Klara are with the Lord. She *will* be judged. Oh! It has been weeks since I have had a companion. I must apologize for talking too much—it has been a vice since I was a child, worsened by the loneliness. There are the orderlies and the cooks, and I have the patients, of course—all these men are companions, but one must be careful, being the only woman, not to let affections develop, lest one follow the sad fate of Sister Klara, and be caught simulating married life in the vestry." Now a blush passed over her face, visible even in the very low light. "Must I say everything at once! You wish to rest. Can I show you to your quarters?"

She looked at him. It was a simple question, but at that moment Lucius could think of nothing other than going home. *How* exactly was beyond him—the hussar was gone, and two days of winter lay between him and the railway station. But certainly there were some means by which he might extricate himself. It was only a matter of explaining: he was not a true doctor yet, the Medical Service had made an error; perhaps with other doctors he could return and help. But alone? No...he couldn't. Certainly, she would understand. Certainly, she was well aware of the incompetence of the High Command, of the growing debacle of a war; certainly she had heard of the entire Third Army sent against the wrong front; certainly she had seen the shoes made of cardboard, the summer coats given to alpine patrols. And if he didn't tell her now, his inexperience would soon become apparent; she would realize it the moment he touched a scalpel...

"Sister..." A pause. But what could he say? *My heartfelt apologies? There has been a mistake? I've never operated, I've cured two patients in my life, one of impacted ear wax and the other of a gonorrhoeal stricture?* Now, standing in the dim light, he could feel not only her eyes, but also the eyes of the soldiers on the floor. *Primum non nocere.* But what did that mean here? Certainly he would do more harm to leave?

They, too, have not asked for this, he thought. *They did not ask to be sent into winter without coats. They, too, were not prepared.* Closest to them, he could see a young man with his head bandaged, staring at him with a single open eye filled with such pleading that Lucius had to look away.

Hope, gratitude, but there was also something else. It was hard to recognize it at first, but then he saw it: a demand—no, an expectation, perhaps even a threat. What would so many injured soldiers do when he told them he couldn't help?

"Pan Doctor?"

He turned back to her. Now his words seemed to come from someone else. "It is important that the patients not be disrupted in their schedules. What was Szökefalvi's custom at this hour?"

"Rounds, Pan Doctor. If there were no emergencies, he would make evening rounds." Her voice soft, her relief palpable, a little constellation of candlelights flickering in what seemed to be her brimming tears.

"Then we should waste no time."

"You will stay then? Even if you feel Her, you will stay?"

Lucius already felt Her. From the moment Margarete began to describe Her, he had felt his skin crawling and had done everything in his power to keep from tearing off his clothes.

"We each have our appointed hour," he mumbled, aware it was something she might say. Something, before this moment, he would never have believed at all.

He shouldered his bag and she led him along one of the paths between the patients. She spoke as they walked. "They are provisionally organized into wards. The nave is where we keep the lesser injuries—the fractures and amputations. We operate within the crossing—the light is best. The south transept is where the dying men are kept, out of sight of the others. The head wounds are in the chancel, where they can be watched." Lanterns hung at even intervals. He was aware now of the walls, painted with scenes from the Bible. An ark, a serpent, crucifixions set amid what seemed to be Carpathian villages, entwined with Latin verse. Gilded saints above the colonnades. A Last Judgment on the sacristy partition, its tree of fire ornamented with monks and hog-tied sinners, marching on a devil's tongue.

At the end of the nave, beneath the Annunciation, they stopped. In the floor of the north transept was a crater, several feet deep. A light dusting of snow covered its walls and the steps of a pulpit. Now he realized that the light he had seen earlier was coming from a jagged hole in the high ceiling, poorly patched with wood and tarpaulin. Sister Margarete said nothing.

"What happened?" he asked, pointing.

As she smiled, the wimple pressed into her cheeks. "What happened, Pan Doctor? Well, there is a hole in the ceiling and a crater in the floor." And she began to laugh as if this was the funniest question she had ever heard.

When he set his bag down by the pulpit, she continued. There were approximately sixty patients in the church of Our Lady of Lemnowice.

Most came from the Third Army, though with regiments garrisoned across the mountains, there were others there as well. The most recent truckload of men had arrived the week before—sixteen soldiers, three dead on arrival, five with wounds requiring immediate amputation. Since then it had been silent. The war had moved off, she said. This was its way. Sometimes the fighting was very close and they could hear gunshots, sometimes only distant shells. Once, the Russians had taken the town. Other times, she wondered if they had been forgotten. What a blessing that would be! The town still had a few people left—women only, Ruthenians whose allegiance likely had once been to Russia, until the Russians had taken all the men when they withdrew. The hospital had enough food to last the winter; in addition to the rations last delivered in mid-January, the church had stores of grain and turnips, sunflower seeds, potatoes, beetroots. As long as supplies continued to come, they could make it through spring, that most difficult of seasons, and come summer there would be apples and pears, and they could work their own fields, and grow wheat…

But Lucius had stopped listening. "Dr Szőkefalvi left in December?"

"December, Doctor."

"Two months ago."

"Yes, two."

"But you just said there have been amputations?"

"Since December, there have been forty amputations, on twenty-three men, Pan Doctor. Eight legs above the knee, fifteen below. Ten arms above the elbow and six below. One jaw that did not survive."

Lucius looked at her, his heart beginning to beat faster. "And who, Sister Margarete, has performed the amputations?"

"*He* has, Pan Doctor," and she rolled her eyes beatifically toward the hole in the north transept.

Lucius did not drop his gaze. "And whose hand was *He* directing, Sister?"

She held up her little hands, scarcely half the span of his.

"And are those patients here?"

"Yes."

"All of them?"

"All that have survived, yes, who have not been evacuated."

"How many have survived, dear Sister?"

"Fourteen have survived, Pan Doctor."

"Fourteen...of twenty-three." He paused, thinking of the Regimental Hospitals in Kraków, the daily removal of corpses. "That is a not a bad survival rate."

"No, Doctor."

"And God has worked by those hands alone?"

A pause, a little smile, as if she understood the impact of what she'd said.

"Sister?"

"God has given us morphine and ether, Doctor."

"Yes," said Lucius, staring. "Yes, yes. He has."

Then she said, "One last thing, Doctor. I have given the men permission to use firearms on the rats, but they must shoot into the floor and not at one another. The typhus, thank God, has abated for now, and we have our procedures for keeping it away. But the rats! Pan Doctor, we are at the mercy of the rats. I have boarded up all the holes in the walls of our church. Sometimes they fall from the hole in the transept, though with winter, this has stopped. Traps have been laid in all corners, but still the creatures come, like mushrooms after a rain, everywhere. You will not be frightened by the occasional shot."

He thought back to her heaving the crossbar in the narthex.

"Is this why you barred the doors, Sister?"

"Oh, no, Pan Doctor. I barred the doors because of the wolves."

THE SECOND DOCTOR SERVICE

Sirs—Having read with interest Dr. Bennett's recent report of the young woman with episodic amnesia and transformation of personality, as well as Dr. Slayer's study "On the So-called Cumberland Were-wolf," I have spent the past months in deliberation over whether to share my own case with your readers. If I have hesitated, it is less out of concern for privacy than the simple fact that, though bearing the title of physician, I am but a country doctor, whose medical expertise extends little beyond those afflictions befalling the farmers and milkmaids of K—County. Indeed, it is likely that I never would have opened your learned *Journal* were it not for the very strange events that have befallen me this past year. Most of the members of your Society, I am aware, publish with that noble aim of advancing medicine; I write with the hope that one of them has encountered a case similar to my own, and so might save me before it is too late.

Unlike with most illnesses, Sirs—which arise within us insidiously, creeping through vein and fiber, unsettling our slumber, gradually awakening within us that ineffable, horrific sense of *dis-ease*—it is possible to state the very *instant,* indeed the very longitude and latitude, of my affliction, being four strokes after Twelve Noon on August 24, 1882, on the cusp of Mersey's Ridge, outside of S—. I was returning from a sick call; the patient was a parson's son who had fallen ill with a tertian fever. I had attended to him for three days and nights with the constant application of Beedham's Ointment and, upon restoring him to health, had saddled my horse and begun my journey home. It was a warm summer day, one of those particularly golden morrows when the air is thick with motes of pollen, and the scent of wet grass rises from the fields, and everywhere life appears to swirl in such a miasma that I have wondered since if I did not inhale some invisible animalcule as I galloped up the hill, and that it is perhaps upon this beastie that I should lay the blame for all that followed. Down in the valley, the noon bells had tolled thrice when there arose a very strong odor of chestnuts, overwhelming the sweet scent of the grass and the sharp bloom of all the goldenrod stirred up by my horse's feet. This was impossible, of course: chestnuts would not be in season until November, and this thought, delivered whole and instantaneously between the third and fourth tolling of the bells, seemed to carry on its wings the conviction that something odd and terrible was to occur. It was then, just as I crested the hill, expecting the spectacular vision of the forests below, that I found myself not before that view, but somehow *five miles farther*, thundering over the bridge at Wilson's Mill.

We are all accustomed, I believe, to the experience of traveling and drifting into distraction, only to arrive safely at our destination as if directed by some unseen hand. My first suspicion was that this was what had happened, and yet I also knew it wasn't so: I had passed along this road a thousand times, and not once had I failed to stop on its descent into that ancient forest of beech and linden, where the soft light filters down through the whispering leaves, and the air is filled with the gay tintinnabulation of the chickadees, and the odor of the mushrooms and mosses never fails to awaken in me a profound nostalgia for my childhood adventures amidst those cathedrals of fallen boughs. Nor, I knew, could I have fallen asleep, for the road is too perilous, with hanging limbs that can dispatch even the most alert traveler. Such is my reasoning in retrospect; at the time it was a particular *sensation* that told me something was different, a feeling, unlike any other I had experienced, of *complete nothingness,* as if an *ellipsis* had occurred between the fields of goldenrod on Mersey's Ridge and the linden depths of the Mill, as if time and distance had somehow *folded* upon themselves, or—to put it differently—as if I had simply ceased to be.

There is little more to be said about this incident, save that it was the first. Shaken, I continued my ride. I stopped at H—to dine, finding myself in the company of an old friend. I made no mention of the event, ate heartily, and, having steadied my nerves, continued home.

For the next two months, nothing happened. I entered my forty-eighth year in the finest of health, save an old toothache and the gout in my right knee. The oaks autumned, followed by the beeches; the parson's boy fell sick again; I rode back and forth over Mersey's Ridge without an incident. In October, I was invited to a Ball in H—, to raise funds for the Deaf School there. Now, since my youth I have dreaded such decorous affairs, preferring the simpler company of my milkmaids and farmers. But the School was dear to Constance, my wife, who has devoted many of her hours to helping those unfortunates. And so it was that I traveled with her to that town, where, in the gaily lit ballroom, I suffered the second of my paroxysms.

Again, I can time the exact moment of the seizure. I was standing in a crowd of doctors and doctors' wives, enduring the rambling braggadocio of a Mission Surgeon who had recently returned from curing Surinam of her hydroceles. He was attempting to shock the ladies, speaking ominously of natives who carted their tuberous scrota about in wheelbarrows, when I noted that same odor of chestnuts and, glancing at the clock, *observed it to advance in one clean stroke* from 7:15 to 7:48. Perplexed, I raised my wineglass to my mouth, only to find it empty. Around me the others, nearly a dozen in number, were watching me, laughing. I was certain I had gaffed. Nervously I looked about the circle, and yet the laugher was welcoming, as if the crowd were eagerly anticipating more. Fortunately, someone rang a bell. Dancing would begin! I turned to Constance, expecting to be scolded. Instead, with a little laugh, a toss of her frizzed bangs, and breath that lifted her bosom against her pale blue bodice, she uttered those words that would prove fatally prescient—*Whatever, Service, has come into you?* Then, with a pleased shiver ruffling the silken rump of her skirts, she led me to the floor.

Of course, I still had no idea what had happened. Dizzied by the absurd notion that I was absent from a conversation in which I had so clearly taken part, I tried to pry the story from Constance as we waltzed. She was happy to rehearse the events—apparently I had given the braggart surgeon quite a humbling, and in such a subtle manner that he had scarcely realized what was happening until it was too late. *Myself,* I thought, humbling *him!* However I might have wished to do such a thing, I don't think I have humbled anyone in my life. The waltz ended, a mazurka started up; though my knee ached, I joined her again if only to collect my thoughts. Of course I immediately associated the attack with the strange occurrence at Mersey's Ridge, for both the sweet aroma that preceded it and that identical sense of a profound, impenetrable void. Clearly, I thought, as the circle turned, I had suffered a *fit*, an *ecstasy*, an *alienation* from my mental faculties. And yet as to the source of this delirium, I remained utterly in the dark. It had neither the wildness of *mania transitoria*, nor the residual symptoms that tend to sift in the wake of an *apoplexy*, nor the violence that accompanies *lycanthropy* and those other perverse transformations of the soul. The premonition of chestnuts, the suddenness of onset, the total lapse of consciousness followed by my precipitous, if slightly stunned, return—all, of course, pointed to epilepsy, if not the *grand mal* of fame, the *larval* or *petit* form, known sometimes simply as the *absence*. But, while not an expert on the nerves, I have attended, twice, to patients diagnosed with this affliction, and while both reported a similar sense of vanishing during their attacks, both *appeared* vacant before the world. Whereas I, apparently, *appeared* to have been possessed by none other than myself.

If I had regarded my first attack with some nonchalance, I found that the second left me with a severe disquiet. Like the tertian of the parson's son, my affliction had declared itself as a form prone to repeat. And while two months separated the first and second attacks, it was but a fortnight before it returned a third time, while I was hunting with my brother Thomas, who'd come from Boston on a visit. Again the attack was heralded by the smell of chestnuts, again the onset was sudden, again the amnesia total. We had spread a blanket out for supper. The dogs lay resting at my feet. I looked up at the sky and saw a distant nimbus, thought, *It will rain*, and then—as if I had summoned the clouds myself—I was on my mount, riding, a heavy rill streaming from the brim of my hat and onto a clutch of four wet quail, their black-grey feathers ruffling with the wind.

I screamed. I could not hold it back. So sudden was the change, so grotesque the bloodied birds! I pulled up my horse. I dismounted. Rain tickled down my collar. I felt a horrid sensation, as if something were fleeing me, some kind of vermin scurrying across my skin. I tore off my coat, my scarf, opened my shirt.

It was then that I caught my brother's eye. Thomas removed his hat, and wiped his sleeve across his forehead. *Richard?* he said. The dogs, too, I saw, were watching, with their own puzzled, canine airs.

Embarrassed, I muttered something, tried to climb back on my horse, slipped and fell into the mud. Thomas dismounted, to de-bog me. Are you ill? he asked.

I shook my head. A swoon, I said. Only nerves! Don't worry, I *am not myself*—that's all.

It was this phrase that did it. A common enough turn, of course: never do we stop to think exactly what it means. But with these words, the slumbering fears that had been with me since my first attack came pouring out. I stuttered out a confession. Thomas listened. He tried to comfort me and denied perceiving any change at all. We'd had a normal lunch, argued heartily about the Wool Tax Repeal, packed our bags, and resumed hunting. Indeed, if there had been any difference, he added with a laugh that was meant to comfort me, *it was for the better;* I even seemed without my typical brooding. A *seizure?* No. He wasn't a medical man, but he'd known many afflicted with seizures. They were all *tumbling fellows,* certainly none had carried on as I did, none had such opinions on the Revenue Code, none—and here he indicated the birds—were such a fine shot.

A fine shot! Sirs, I have, in my life, never been "a fine shot." Whether it is a mild tremor, or a fondness for Nature's gentler creatures, something always seems to unsteady my hand when I attempt to pull the trigger. I go hunting for love of the out-of-doors, for the manly company, for the beneficial effects of fresh air on the lungs, and if I have returned with bounty, it is only out of luck. Thus while four quail in a single afternoon might have been welcomed by most, for me it came as a terrifying aberration. I was *not* myself; something *had* come into me, and if no change was observed in my countenance, this was not proof of the intruder's clemency, but rather the sophistication of his deception. By then I had spent enough time in our County Association Library in search of insight into my condition to know about the violence man commits in altered states. I speak of the district-court judge who, seizing, would rise at his supper and, with the clatter of silverware trailing in his wake, commence such a devastation that his family had no choice but to employ a strongman to wrestle him into submission. Or the case reported by Hoyle of the somnambulist who awoke to find himself dining on raw meat from the icebox. Or the virtuous young lady of Northampton who, in fits of insanity, would seek congress with chimney sweeps and rag mongers. Or the young schoolteacher-turned-murderer who, following his execution, was found to have a massive tumor of the temporal lobe. Or Pritchard's epileptic, who woke with magpies in his pockets and *with no such memory of what had occurred.*

Can you imagine, Sirs, what it is like to pass one's hours like this, waiting, knowing that at any moment you will be transformed? That you could retire to the sitting room, only to find yourself standing among the shards of your treasured china, blood on your hands, some leering ragman on your flanks? I feared each new smell, every shiver of wind. The seizures were massing, I knew. As if I were some kind of monstrous human Leyden jar, the current gathering force until it was ready to discharge. And discharge it did, with ever increasing frequency. At dinner, I lifted a piece of ham to my mouth only to find myself swallowing pudding. I tossed my grandson in the air, and caught my dimpled, giggling granddaughter. I began Genesis 25 and finished Exodus 12. I unsheathed the knife I used for my Caesarians and found myself with a bonneted baby in my arms. But no matter how complete the *alienation,* there was no crime, no *morbid* transformation. When I inspected the surgical sites repaired by my Imposter, there was not a stitch awry. By every account, I was very much the same man; indeed, Constance confirmed what my brother had noted: this second Dr. Service was perhaps a subtle *improvement* on the first. *He* didn't lick his comb. *He* didn't swear, *he* didn't clean *his* nostrils by advancing his handkerchief into them; if he spit, it was done in small volumes, with good aim, and without noisy preamble. He was even—I learned after a seizure struck while I was being photographed at the annual meeting of the County Association—ever so slightly handsomer: less stooped, with a "twinkle" in the eye and a smile befitting the confidence of a man who has a secret to confide. As to the nature of this secret, I could only wonder; it wasn't long, however, before I suspected its relation to a new flush in Constance's cheeks, a new limpid depth to her gaze—a suspicion, Sirs, which filled my heart with man's most ancient envy, an envy unmitigated by the realization that the cuckold and the cuckoo were the same.

Let me return, though, to the County Association photograph. How many hours I spent staring at it! I don't know what, exactly, I was seeking, save that somewhere in his visage I expected to find an explanation of who he...I...*we*...were. He wore *my* black overcoat and *my* top hat and *my* silken grey ascot, which Constance had given me for my birthday. His mustache was waxed into the sharpest arabesque (mine was in the "natural" style). While the velvet collar of *my* overcoat had a tendency to accumulate all forms of detritus, his was finely brushed; the satin of the hat almost glistened. But it was into the eyes that I found myself staring. The more I studied them, the more I perceived, beyond their gay façade, something more profound, that perplexity and quiet sadness that one often encounters in the eyes of those who have struggled with the mysteries of the world. Indeed, the more I considered it, the more I came to think that however strange this *possession* had been for me, it must have been so much stranger for him. A babe, you will admit, is spared the horror of its birth by virtue of its stupidity. It need not ask where it comes from, or whether the sun will rise tomorrow, or what will become of its soul when the worms descend upon its flesh. And yet the second Dr. Service was forced to take up the very reins of life that morning of his awakening on Mersey's Ridge. Was he born, then, knowing how to ride? If so, are we all conceived with infinite capabilities? Such that what man calls Learning is actually a winnowing of inborn wisdom? Is it the newborn who is the true sage, while the figure of the wise old man is but an illusion perpetrated by his whiskers and his cane?

Or perhaps he hadn't been so immaculately conceived. Had he come from elsewhere? Was this less a possession than a collision, a stone skipping across a pond, an errant soul in transmigration, who had the misfortune of landing not in a newborn but a man of forty-eight, with his melancholies and his gouty knees?

Or was he I, divided? A cutting which, cleaved from the stock, goes on to send forth its own roots? Or the corybantic twitching of a severed lizard's tail, which eventually grows still? Were my memories his? What happens, Sirs, to the essence of the sea cucumber when the sea cucumber is cut in two?

The more I pondered my condition, the more such questions gave onto others, budded, and bred, until they churned with such violence inside my mind that I had to do something to set them free. But to whom was I to turn? When I dared speak of my illness to Constance, she could scarcely hide her irritation. By then, she too had been transformed, into a raven-eyed Messalina who endured her *first* husband as if *he*—I!—were the aberration. My brother was in Boston. I dared not approach another physician lest he commit me to an asylum against my will.

This left only my double. I contrived, therefore, to seek him out directly, tucking about my person various inquires, in the hope that during my paroxysms, he might place his hand into my coat pocket, discover one of the missives, and in turn reply regarding who he was, and where he had come from, and—and this I added only with hesitation— *what he would become.* Constance, driven to fury by the scraps, which inevitably made their way into her possession, begged me to stop. So I had experienced a change, she said. What of it? Such is the way of life; we are never the same people we once were. Enough! she pleaded. Think what would happen if the authorities discover you! You will lose your patients, your practice, your...*our*...home.

But by then I did not care. By then, with winter drawing on, I'd experienced, for the first time, two seizures in the course of a single day. I *needed* to reach him, if only to strike some kind of entente. I begged, I reasoned, my thoughts bubbled onto my lips. I reminded him that it was I who gave him life. I haggled, offering him all he wanted if he would only swear to continue granting my return. I warned him of the fate of the parasite that mistakenly destroys its host.

Nothing. No reply. No word of comfort. No tearstain of fellow suffering on my lines of ink. Everywhere, I found myself surrounded by the creeping evidence of his passage: the fingerprints on the crystal Constance told me to reserve for visitors, the tooth marks on my pipe stem, those humid sheets. But still he remained deaf to my entreaties. Deaf, Sirs—and then one evening in December, on the top shelf of my library, a sheath of papers caught my gaze. I can still recall my trembling hands as I climbed the bookcase ladder, certain I had found that long-awaited letter from my other half. And yet, as I brought the pages into the light, I found to my surprise what appeared to be a novel. It was unfinished, with corrections scattered over the manuscript, and if not the confession I'd hoped for, it was proof, nonetheless, that "R. Servus, Or: the Slave," as the author called himself, did not live a life of naïve indifference, but grappled, as I did, with the puzzling mystery of his transformation.

It was a long work—I do not have time to set down all the details here. I will distill it to the following: a young nobleman named Gaspard, after years of dissolution, meets, like Goethe, his double riding down a wintry path. But while the German's famous vision vanished as soon as it appeared, the protagonist of Servus's tale rides for a while *with* his doppelgänger, the latter telling him the story of the life he led up to the moment of their meeting. The second Gaspard's story is oddly similar to the first, if even a bit lustier, culminating in the night when he (the second Gaspard), returning from his mistress's castle, meets *his* double on a mountain road. We are then treated to what seems to be the story of a third Gaspard, except this time familiar details begin to suggest themselves, and with a chill, we realize, as the first Gaspard does, that he is being told the story of his own life, through that same wintry night when he meets his double on the road. And as the second Gaspard continues to speak, the first Gaspard begins to feel a terror growing in his heart, a remembrance that the vision of one's double is said to be an omen of impending death. At that moment, *driven by a force not his own,* he reaches into his cloak and finds a dagger—a black dagger with a ruby in its hilt—a dagger he never owned!—leaps from his horse and—

But as I turned the page, I found only blank paper. I turned back, suspecting the final page had adhered to its predecessor, but there was nothing. Frantic then, I redoubled my search, extracting volume after volume from my shelves, finding nothing other than those scraps that bore my own pathetic queries. It was nearly dawn. I began to feel ill— my head ached—I knew with certainty that the fate of Gaspard held the secret to my own. The violence of the novel, that final terrifying image of the strange dagger, could not but foretell a bloody finale. Surely, I thought, the first Gaspard would kill the second! But then what? Would he find himself exorcised of the demon? Or, the moment he plunged the blade into the Other's heart, would he feel its cold steel enter his own? What fantasy did my shadow live out on these pages? Was this a fear? A threat? Until that day I thought him indifferent to my existence, and if not indifferent, at the very least curious, maybe grateful, maybe even sorry for the man from whose head, Athena-like, he'd sprung. Now I knew it wasn't so. This was why the squatter had never answered my entreaties. He *wished* me to go mad! To lose my mind so that *he* might gain it. I was his enemy, his rotting limb, *his* parasite, the dying master of the kingdom he would one day rule.

By then, Constance was knocking at my door. I gathered up the scattered pages. She couldn't know! There was no hope in trying to explain—she would never believe—she would insist I wrote it. No, it was more insidious: *she already knew.* That was it, I realized, with horror: she *knew,* she was *waiting* for me to go, so as to welcome that usurper completely to her bed. I smelled chestnuts—I leapt up to hide the volume—*he, they* couldn't know I'd found it—I gained the ladder—I felt a wind—I cried out briefly—and then his tongue choked back my own.

I awoke in our carriage, gliding across the winter fields. Constance was sleeping, and for the longest time, I knew not where we were.

And so I find myself. Sirs, if I write to you now with some composure, if my pen is steady, if my words measured—Sirs, if this seems so, you must trust me when I say that it was but weeks ago that you would not have recognized me for the wild phrensy with which I fought my fate. Oh, I was like the drowning man who, gasping, bursts from placid waters, only to be pulled back in. Every ounce of my force was devoted to *his* destruction. (There were three of us then: Servus and I, and the terror that drove me to destroy him.) I didn't sleep—no: slumber I would leave for he-I-hatched. I paced, I muttered, ranted, raced my mare into the fiercest storms, only to find myself awake in my reading chair, at home, with some gentle volume open on my lap. On cliffs, I galloped, waiting for the seizure that would send *him* tumbling to the earth. I tried to maim him. I held needles to my eye, hoping that with my seizure, he would twitch. I noosed my rope—he retained me. I lit a match—he blew it out. With my razor, I touched the twinned pulse of our carotids, the beat of our eight-chambered heart. His hand clasped mine. My tears fell from his eyes.

I had no February, Sirs.

And now I am grown tired. (A week separates these lines.)

Servus thrives. With each convulsion I wake to find myself a less familiar man. Empty grouse and rag-stuffed staghorns decorate the place that I once called my home. Coming to, I feel hunting songs fading from my lips, their tunes briefly crossing our threshold before dying out. Sometimes, awaking with the brush of Constance's breath against my cheek, I believe, briefly, that I have returned to stay, only to be swept away again for weeks. Strangely, I am no longer afraid. Have I reconciled myself to my fate? Or is this simply the course of my affliction? Having claimed my wife, my February, now my April, has he now come to take my fears? Or is it simply that my lucid intervals, like the briefest of encores, are too ephemeral for terror to take hold? I know not. Perhaps you, Gentlemen, can tell me. For now, I hasten to the post, lest Cain appear and confiscate this cry. I pray that if I am to lose my June, my August—if the year turns before I awake—I still might one day find your answer in the dusty journals of the County Association Library. Or will you too abandon me? Will you dismiss me as but a seizure in *his* mind? Will you rejoice, Sirs, as he advances, steadily, toward cure?

Q&A WITH DANIEL MASON

JUNE 2020: *ZYZZYVA*

REGAN MCMAHON

After publishing three novels, *The Piano Tuner* (2002), *A Far Country* (2005), and *The Winter Soldier* (2018), Bay Area author Daniel Mason released his first collection of short fiction in May, *A Registry of My Passage Upon the Earth*. As he does in his longer works, he takes us into the minds and hearts of complex, nuanced characters and places them in intricately described settings, often in the natural word, detailed with the depth and precision of a botanist or anthropologist. He is, in fact, a man of science—by day he's a clinical assistant professor in the Stanford University Department of Psychiatry. He wrote his first book, *The Piano Tuner*, while still in medical school at UC San Francisco.

Mason lives in his hometown of Palo Alto with his wife, novelist Sara Houghteling, and their two young boys. His work has been translated into twenty-eight languages. *The Piano Tuner* was adapted for an opera in 2004, and a film adaptation is in development. Last month he received the 2020 Joyce Carol Oates Prize, a $50,000 award from the Simpson Literary Project. The prize is given annually to a mid-career fiction author, who normally spends a limited residency at Cal the following spring, working with college and graduate students, and makes appearances at Simpson Project writing workshops for Bay Area teenagers (offered at no charge). This is the fourth year of the prize. I served on the jury the first year, so I know how rigorous the selection process is.

How did you feel when you learned that you'd won the Joyce Carol Oates Prize? How will it affect your life?

I was both honored and quite surprised. Writing is such a private experience—it is surreal to me to realize that someone has read my writing closely, let alone a jury or a writer like Joyce Carol Oates, whom I have been reading for thirty years. As for how it will affect my life, the honest answer is I don't know right now. We are in such a tumultuous time—on a practical matter, the pandemic has made something as simple as a research trip very difficult; on a larger scale Covid, and the protests and reexamination of American history sparked by the killing of George Floyd, have all affected how I think about my writing in the world. I do love the community engagement aspect of the Joyce Carol Oates Prize, and I hope that the pandemic risk will subside enough for me to participate with the schools.

You're known for historical fiction, but I noticed on the Simpson Literary Project website you said, "My writing has increasingly turned toward this current time, and I will use the prize to continue new work set here in California." Can you tell us some of your California story ideas?

A Registry of My Passage upon the Earth contains one story—"For the Union Dead"—which is set in California, and it was fascinating to me to look at the place I was born and have lived in for most of my life. Several new stories, and the early stages of a novel are also set here. The natural world—our oceans, our flora, our fires—all play a central role in all of them.

Lots of writers have day jobs, but yours is as a practicing psychiatrist and professor. Are you a doctor who writes fiction, or a fiction writer who's a doctor? Are you the same person in both roles? Or is there an intrinsic tension/dialectic at play? What is the difference between diagnosis and character creation?

This has changed over time—at first, it felt like inhabiting two different people, now I feel more like the same person. There are so many overlaps between the two fields. Diagnosis may ultimately be a process of distillation, but to get there, we need narrative. This may be just a simple story, but it usually is much more complex, taking in account of a patient's work, family, childhood, fears, wishes. This process feels a lot like storytelling. When I write, I constantly ask whether I am missing something, how I can make a character more real, who else is in their world, what questions would bring them more fully to life.

Your characters seem especially introspective. Does being a psychiatrist give you a particular empathy and imagination regarding other people's minds?

I'm not sure if being a psychiatrist gives me any more empathy than other writers. After all, my favorite writers of the internal world are not psychiatrists, so it means this is hardly a precondition. If there is a connection, I think it is this sense that human beings are mysteries. Since I was young, human beings have always been puzzling to me. If anything, this interest drove me toward both fields…

The stories in your new collection were written over a long period of time. Together, do they represent your personal journey over time, or your growth as a writer? Are there any autobiographical details in the stories?

There are many autobiographical details—when I went back to look at them, I'm struck by how personal they are. Alfred Russel Wallace's wonder at the natural world is my wonder (his endurance is more of an aspiration, rather than a reality for me). [The story, about the British naturalist who independently of Darwin conceived of natural selection, is titled "The Ecstasy of Alfred Russel Wallace."] The worry of the mother in "On Growing Ferns" is my worry for my children in a future of climate change. The balloonist in "On the Cause of Winds and Waves" confronts the boundary of fiction and creation which I find myself living in whenever I write. In "The Line Agent Pascal," the main character finds connection with others despite extraordinary isolation—I think the core of this comes from wondering about how people forge different lives that still have deep meaning, something I think about often outside of my writing.

You didn't become a fiction writer or hone your skills by going through an MFA program, as many novelists have. When did you fall in love with words? When did you know you were a writer?

I would read constantly when I was a child—I can still remember leaning on my bed, knees on the floor, like some kind of archetypal position of bedtime prayer. I also wrote—little stapled books and stories for myself, school contests, etc. And in college I took a writing course with the wonderful Jill McCorkle. But I never really knew what to do with this interest until I started writing *The Piano Tuner*, very much accidentally, and it occurred to me as I approached the end that it might actually be a book. But even then, the idea of publishing it somewhere seemed inconceivable.

Detailed descriptions of the natural world are a big part of many of your stories and novels. Have you been influenced by any nature writers or travel writers?

Both Tolstoy and Melville are of course so much more than nature writers, but if you stripped their books of everything but the natural descriptions, I think you would be left with the most vivid nature writing in literature. I also love older classics of travel—Wallace, Darwin, [Henry Walter] Bates, [Richard] Spruce. Then there are writers who aren't explicitly nature writers, but who organize their narratives around movement through physical space, like W.G. Sebald. I also read field guides obsessively, a habit that began almost twenty years ago, first with plant guides, then fungi and lichens; now it's spiders. There is something I love so much about technical description, the drive to create in words something that exists in the world, the way a creature appears in the mind, the vocabulary. There is a thrill of being forty-four years old and encountering whole books of English words that I have never used, or even encountered before…chelicerae, pedipalps, spinnerets…

Do you approach writing short fiction any differently than you do a novel? Have you ever written a story and thought it deserved to be expanded to a novel? Or conversely, thought you had a great premise for a novel and then decided you'd tell that story in a more compact way?

I realize that despite the fact that I've been doing this for twenty years, I still don't know. There is a certain quality to an idea or image which suggests a shorter arc—my novel ideas have tended to appear as much messier worlds. It is harder to articulate more than this though. None of my novels have come out of short stories, and none of my abandoned novels (and there have been many) became short stories. Many of my stories in this collection were ideas from years ago, that sat there waiting until for some reason, the story itself emerged.

Your stories have so much precise detail, descriptions, and vocabulary— from The Piano Tuner's *description of the mechanics of pianos and malarial hallucinations, to the insect specimens in this collection's "The Ecstasy of Alfred Russel Wallace." By the time I got to the final, title story of* A Registry of My Passage Upon the Earth, *about the real-life schizophrenic artist Arthur Bispo de Rosário, who catalogued and organized every experience and object he had, it hit me that in a way, that's what you do: give readers all the detail and information about a character and his or her place, and leave it to us to make sense of it. Do you relate to his obsession?*

It's wonderful that you noticed this. I very much relate to him; I feel he articulates something so fundamental about the act of creation itself: the drive to discover and record something, to capture something beautiful or strange about the world, to turn it over in one's hands and then set out to make something with it, a memento, something that could say "I experienced this…I was here."

MASTIFF

JOYCE CAROL OATES

Earlier on the trail, they'd seen it. The massive dog.

Tugging at its master's leash so that the young man's calves bulged with muscle as he held the dog back. Grunting what sounded like *Damn Rob-roy! Damn dog* in a tone of exasperated affection.

Signs on the trail forbade dogs without leashes. At least, the massive dog was on a leash.

The woman stared at the dog not twelve feet away wheezing and panting. Its head was larger than her own, with a pronounced black muzzle, bulging glassy eyes. Its jaws were powerful, and slack; its lips shone, and the large long tongue rosy-pink as a sexual organ dripped slobber. The dog was pale-brindle-furred, with a deep chest, muscled shoulders and legs, a short taut tail. It might have weighed two hundred pounds. Its panting was damply audible, unsettling. The straggly-bearded young man who gripped the leather leash with both hands, in beige hoodie, multi-pocketed khaki shorts, hiking boots, squinted at the woman, and at the man behind her, with an expression that might have been apologetic, or defensive; or maybe, the woman thought, the young man was laughing at them, ordinary hikers without a massive monster-dog tugging and straining at their arms.

The woman thought *That isn't a dog. It's a human being on his hands and knees. That face!*

Such surreal thoughts bombarded the woman's brain waking and sleeping. So long as no one else could know the woman paid little heed.

Fortunately, the massive dog and its master were taking another hiking trail into Wild Cat Canyon. Eagerly the dog lunged forward sniffing at the ground, the young man following with muttered curses.

The woman felt relief, the ugly dog hadn't attacked her! She and her male companion continued on the main trail which was approximately two and a half miles uphill to Wild Cat Canyon Peak.

The man, sensing the woman's unease at the sight of the dog, made some joke which the woman didn't quite hear and did not acknowledge. They were walking single file, the woman in the lead. She waited for the man to touch her shoulder as another man might have done to comfort but she knew that he would not, and he did not. The man said, in a tone of slight reproof, that the dog was an English mastiff—"Beautiful dog."

The woman felt the man's remark as a rebuke of a kind. Much of what the man said to the woman she understood was in rebuke of her narrow judgment, her timorous ways. Sometimes, the woman amused the man, for these reasons. At other times, the woman annoyed the man and she saw in his gentlemanly face an expression of startled disapproval, veiled contempt. She thought *He sees through me. My subterfuge, my ignorance. My desperation.*

The woman said, over her shoulder, with a wild little laugh, "Yes! Beautiful."

The hike that day to Wild Cat Canyon Peak would be a hike uphill, into the sun. Splotched light and shadow on the trail, momentary spells of sun-blindness. The woman was thrilled to be outdoors, and hiking with the man. *This* man, to whom she'd been introduced with great promise seven weeks, four days before at a dinner party in a mutual friend's home in the north Berkeley hills.

The hike had been the man's suggestion. Or, rather, in his oblique way, which might have been (the woman thought) a strategy of shyness, like her own, he'd simply told her that he was going hiking that weekend, and would she like to join him?

In this way, the man had not risked being rejected. The woman had been made to know that if she came with him she was accompanying *him.*

The woman and the man had gone on walks together, by this time. But a hike of such ambition, to Wild Cat Canyon Peak, seemed to the woman something very different.

She'd said, with her wild little laugh, "Yes! I'd love that."

~

It was late afternoon. Several hours the man and the woman had been hiking. And now single file down the mountain from Wild Cat Canyon Peak they were making their careful way. The woman was descending first, then the man. For the man was the more experienced hiker and wanted to watch over the woman whom he didn't trust not to hurt herself. She'd surprised him by insisting upon wearing lightweight women's running shoes on the trail and not, as he was wearing, hiking boots.

She hadn't thought to bring water, either. The man carried a twelve-ounce plastic bottle of water for them both.

The man had been amused by the woman. Just possibly, the man had been a little annoyed by the woman.

Yet, he was drawn to the woman. He hoped to like her more than he did—he hoped to adore her. For he'd been so very lonely for too long and had come to bitterly resent the solitude of his life.

At the outset of the hike it had been an unnaturally balmy day in late March. At midday, the temperature might have been as high as sixty-eight-degrees F. Now as the sun sank in the western sky like a broken bloody egg darkness and cold began to lift from the earth. The man had suggested to the woman that she bring along a light canvas jacket in her backpack, he knew how quickly the mountain trail could turn cold in the late afternoon, but the woman had worn just a pullover sweater, jeans, and a sun-visor hat more appropriate for summer. (The woman's eyes were sensitive to sunlight even with sunglasses. She hated how easily they watered, tears running down her cheeks like an admission of female weakness.) She'd confounded the man by not bringing any backpack at all with the excuse that she hated feeling "burdened."

Now in the gathering chill the woman was shivering. If she hadn't clenched her jaws tight, her teeth would have chattered.

The trail had looped upward through pine woods to a spectacular view at Wild Cat Canyon Peak where a stone monument had been erected to the early twentieth-century environmentalist landowner who'd left many thousands of acres of land to the State of California for the park. Then, the trail looped down, in tortuous switchbacks, to the trailhead an hour's hike away, and the parking lot which would be "gated," as signs warned, at 6:00 p.m. It was already 4:40 p.m.

At the peak, the man had taken photographs with his new camera while the woman gazed out into the distance, at the spectacular view. At the horizon was a rim of luminous blue—the Pacific Ocean miles away. In the near distance were small lakes, streams. The hills were strangely sculpted, like those bald hills in the paintings of Thomas Hart Benton.

The man had given the woman water to drink. Though she'd said she wasn't thirsty, he'd insisted. There's a danger of dehydration when you've been exerting yourself, he said. Sternly he spoke, like a parent you could not reasonably oppose.

The man spoke with the confidence of one who is rarely challenged. At times the woman quite liked this air of authority, at other times she resented it. The man seemed always to be regarding the woman with a bemused air like a scientist confronted with a curious specimen. She didn't want to think—(yet she thought, compulsively)—that he must be comparing her with other women he'd known, and was finding her lacking.

At the peak, absorbed in his photography, the man seemed to have forgotten the woman. How childlike, how self-contained and maddening! The woman had never been so at repose in her *self*.

For nearly an hour the man would linger at the peak, taking photographs. During this time other hikers came and went. It was no effort for the woman to speak with these hikers briefly while the man seemed oblivious of them. It wasn't his way, he'd told the woman, to strike up conversations with "random" persons. Why not, she'd asked, and he'd said, with a look that suggested that her question was virtually incomprehensible to them, *Why not? Because I'll never see them again.*

With her provocative little laugh the woman said *But that's the best reason for talking to strangers—you will never see them again.*

At least the straggly-bearded young man with the massive dog—the English mastiff—hadn't climbed to the top of Wild Cat Canyon Peak.

But other hikers with dogs made their way there. A succession of dogs, in fact, of all sizes and breeds, fortunately most of them well-behaved and disinclined to bark; several trailing their masters, older dogs, looking chastised, winded. The damp subdued eyes of these older dogs seemed to seek the woman's own eyes.

"Nice dog! What's his name?"

Or, she'd ask, with widened eyes, "What breed is he?"

The woman understood that her male companion had taken note of her fear of the mastiff, at the start of the hike. How she'd tensed at the sight of the ugly wheezing beast that had to be the largest dog of its kind she'd ever seen, nearly as large as a St. Bernard, but totally lacking the benign shaggy aura of the St. Bernard. How she'd stared at the slobbering jaws and glassy blind-seeming eyes—as if in recognition of something not to be named.

And so at Wild Cat Canyon Peak the woman made it a point to engage dog owners in conversations, in her bright airy friendly way. She'd asked about their dogs, she'd even petted the gentler ones.

As a child of nine or ten she'd been attacked by a fierce-barking German shepherd. She'd done nothing to provoke the attack and could remember only screaming and trying to run as the dog barked furiously at her and snapped at her bare legs. Only the intervention of adults had saved her, she'd thought.

The woman hadn't told the man much about her life. Not yet. And possibly never. Her principle was *Never reveal your weakness.*

Especially to strangers, this was essential. *Never reveal your weakness.*

In a technical manner of speaking the woman and the man were "lovers" but they were not intimate. You might say—(the woman might have said)—that they were strangers, essentially.

The woman liked to say to her friends, to amuse them, that she wanted not *to marry* but to *be married.* She wanted a relationship that seemed already mature, if not old and settled, at the start. Newness and rawness did not appeal to her.

"Excuse me? When do you think we might leave?"—hesitantly the woman spoke to the man, not liking to interrupt his concentration.

In their relationship, the woman had not yet displayed any impatience. The woman had not raised her voice, not once.

At last, the man put away his camera, which was a heavy, complicated instrument, into his backpack. And the water bottle, which contained just two or three inches of water—"We might need this, later." The man's movements were measured and deliberate as if he were alone and the woman felt a sudden stab of dislike for him, that he took such care with trivial matters, and yet did not love her.

There were no restrooms on the damned trail—of course. These were serious hiking trails, for serious hikers. Longingly the woman recalled the restroom facilities at the trailhead, a considerable distance downhill. How long would it take, to hike back down? Another hour? For male hikers stopping to urinate in the woods was no great matter; for female hikers, an effort and an embarrassment. Not since she'd been a young girl trapped on a hateful long hike in summer camp in the Adirondacks, had she been forced to relieve herself in the woods. The memory was hazy and blurred with shame, and humiliation at the very pettiness of the discomfort. If she'd told this to the man he would have laughed at her.

Driving to the park that day, the man and the woman had felt very happy together. It sometimes happened to them, unpredictably—a sudden flaring-up of happiness, even joy, in each other's company. The man had been unusually talkative. The woman laughed at his remarks, surprised that he could be so witty. She'd been flattered that, a few days before, he'd visited her art gallery, and had purchased a small soapstone sculpture.

The woman had slid over in the passenger's seat, to sit closer to the man, as a young girl might do, impulsively. How natural this felt, a rehearsal of intimacy!

They'd spent time together in the woman's house, upstairs in her bed—but they hadn't yet spent an entire night together. The man felt self-conscious in the woman's house, the woman felt as if the man were a house-guest, to be treated graciously and not intimately. She hadn't been able to sleep yet beside the man for the physical fact of him was so distracting, he took up too much space in her bed. Naked and horizontal, the man seemed much larger than he did clothed and vertical. He breathed loudly, wetly, through his opened mouth, and though he woke affably when she nudged him, the woman had not wanted to wake him often. She'd resigned herself to lying awake, listening to him breathe. Yet, her physical discomfort was acute—*I can't sleep, I will never sleep if this man is in my bed.*

The woman had not ever been comfortable with a man in close quarters, unless she'd been drinking. But the man scarcely drank. And the woman no longer lost herself in drink, that life was behind her.

On the car radio a piano piece by the Czech composer Janáček—the title was translated "In the Mists." The woman recognized the composition within a few notes. She'd played the piano cycle years ago as a girl. Her eyes filled with tears as she remembered.

Through the somber, distinctive piano notes in a minor—"misty"—key the man continued talking, as if he didn't hear the music. Avidly the woman listened to the piano notes and not to the man's words but the man's voice was suffused with the melancholy beauty of the music and she felt how she loved him, or might love him.

He will be the one. It's time.

The woman was forty-one years old. The man was several years older, she believed. The two had been introduced by a mutual friend, closer emotionally to the man than to the woman, who'd said to the man *You will like Mariella. You will like her face* and to the woman *Simon is an extraordinary person but that might not be evident immediately. Give him time.*

The man had been the director of a distinguished research laboratory in Berkeley, California for many years. His work was predominant in his life. Scientific truth was sacrosanct, unassailable, as it was impersonal and transcendent. His work was what he'd leave behind of himself. He was idealistic, a zealot for science education and the preservation of the environment. He was famously generous with younger scientists. He was a legendary mentor to his graduate students and post-docs. He'd never married. He wasn't sure he'd ever been *in love*. He had no children, though he'd always wanted children. He was dissatisfied with his life, outside the lab. He felt cheated and foolish, that others might pity him. Especially those younger colleagues whom he'd helped in their careers.

He'd been disturbed earlier that year, visiting one of his protégées at the Salk Institute who was married, had several children, and a scientist-wife; the young family lived in a split-level cedar house on three acres of wooded land. In this household the man had felt sharply the emptiness in his own life, in the under-furnished rented house near the University in which he'd lived for more than twenty years, imagining a kind of pride since, from this house, he could so easily bicycle or walk to the lab.

He'd gone away from the young family's house shaken and shattered. And not long afterward, he'd been introduced to the woman of whom it was said *You will like Mariella's face.*

The woman was also lonely and dissatisfied, but it was others with whom she was primarily dissatisfied, not herself. She'd had intense relationships with men since college but invariably she'd been involved with several men at the same time, seeing them simultaneously so that she was prevented from feeling much emotion for any of them. At the same time, she was deeply hurt if a man wasn't involved exclusively with *her*. She'd seen her mother obsequious in her marriage. Her tall handsome father hadn't valued the wife who'd humbled herself for him; he'd left her, when the woman had been a child, and he'd rarely visited his children. All her life she'd yearned for the absent man even as she'd resented him. Her fantasy was her father returning, and she and her mother spurning him with gales of wild laughter.

She'd thought *It's insane to be vulnerable, as women are. Nothing is worth such hurt.*

Yet, she was an attractive woman. Within a small circle of friends she was highly popular, admired. She dressed stylishly. She had many social activities. She'd invested wisely in an art gallery. Despite this, much of her mental life was preoccupied with how she appeared in others' eyes. She could barely force herself to contemplate her image in a mirror: far from beautiful, not even pretty, her face too small, heart-shaped, her chin too narrow, her eyes too large and deep-set. She hated it, she was *petite*. She'd have liked to be five feet ten inches tall, to walk with an air of female swagger, sexual confidence. At five feet three inches, she had no choice but to be the recipient, the very receptacle, of a man's desire.

It disturbed her that she was so detached from her family, her relatives and girlhood friends. In the midst of a buoyant social occasion something inside the woman seemed to switch off. She could feel the deadness seeping into her, the chill indifference. Her women friends close as sisters hugging her, kissing her at the end of an evening, a friend's husband male slipping his arm around her waist to kiss her, just a little too hard, with too much vehemence— "Goodnight, Mariella!" And the coldness in her responded *I don't give a damn if I ever see any of you again.*

She laughed at herself, such emptiness. A hole in the heart.

She could have wept. She would soon be forty-two years old.

Yet it happened, in the new man's company, the woman felt a rare hopefulness. If she couldn't love the man it might be enough for the man to love *her*; enough for them to have a child together, at least.

(What would the man have thought, if he'd known how the woman plotted? Or were these harmless fantasies, not likely to be realized?)

(In the woman's weakest moments, she lamented that she had no children; she would soon be too old for children. Yet, young children bored her, even her young nieces and nephews who she conceded were beautiful.)

Now, making her way down the trail, eager to be out of the park that had seemed so beautiful hours ago, the woman was feeling disconsolate. The long rest at the peak had enervated her. The man's indifference had enervated her. As the sun shifted in the sky so she felt strength leaking from her.

Brooding and silent the man was walking behind the woman, sometimes so close he nearly trod upon her heels. She wanted to turn to scream at him— "Don't do that! I'm going as quickly as I can."

So absorbed was the woman in the voice inside her head she only half-realized she'd been hearing a familiar sound from somewhere close by—a wet chuffing noise, as of labored breathing. The trail continued to drop, turning back upon itself; another, lower trail ran parallel with it now, and would join with it within a few yards, and on this trail two figures were hurrying, one of them, in the lead, a large beast running on all fours.

The woman heard panting ahead. A sensation of fear washed over her.

She had no choice but to blunder forward. Appalled, she saw the massive dog ahead, unavoidable. The damp shining eyes were fixed upon her, not blind-seeming now, but sharply focused. With a kind of canine indignation quickly shifting to fury the dog barked at the stricken woman, straining at his leash as the straggly-bearded young man shouted for the dog to *sit*.

The woman knew better than to succumb to panic, certainly the woman knew better than to provoke the massive dog. It is always a mistake to expose one's weakness. Her terror of what those teeth and sharp claws could do to her.

She couldn't help herself—she screamed, and shrank away. It was the worst possible reaction to the dog that, maddened by the woman's terror, leapt at her, loudly barking and growling, wrenching the leash out of his master's hands.

In an instant the mastiff was on the woman, snarling and biting, nearly knocking her onto the ground. Even in her terror the woman was thinking *My face. I must protect my face.*

Behind her, the man quickly intervened. He seemed to her fearless, astonishing—pulling her back, behind him, shouting at the dog's master to call the damned dog off.

Futilely the young man was shouting—"Rob-*roy!* Rob-*roy!*" The dog paid not the slightest heed to his master, viciously attacking the man, on its hind legs and pummeling him as if to knock him down, that it might tear at his throat with its bared, yellowish fangs.

The frantic struggle could not have lasted more than a few seconds. Fiercely the man tried to shove the dog away, striking it with his bare fists, kicking at it. The straggly-bearded young man yanked at the dog's collar, cursing. With great effort he managed to pull the furious dog away from the man who was bleeding badly from lacerations on his hands and arms and face.

The man had been knocked to one knee. The dog might have torn out his throat but the young man yanked back hard, as if to break the dog's neck.

The terrified woman was cringing behind the man. Always she would remember how unhesitatingly the man had leapt forward to protect her, taking no heed for his own safety.

In the confusion of the struggle, the woman felt something warm on her face. Not blood but the dog's loathsome slobber.

The dog's master managed to extricate the dog from the couple. Still it was barking hysterically, lunging and leaping with bared fangs.

The woman cried, "Help him! Get help for him! He'll bleed to death."

The young man apologized profusely. He was holding the struggling down with both arms. Claiming the dog had never done anything like this before—not ever... "Jesus! I'll get help." There was a ranger station a half-mile down the trail, the young man said. He'd run, he'd get help from the rangers.

Alone with the injured man, the woman cradled him in her arms as he moaned and writhed with pain. He appeared to be dazed, stupefied. Was he in shock? His skin felt cold to the woman's touch. She could barely comprehend what had happened, and so swiftly.

The crazed dog had bitten and scratched her hands, too. There were cuts and abrasions in her flesh, bleeding. But her fear was for the man. She fumbled for her cell phone, tried to call 911 but the call failed to go through. She wondered—should she try to make a tourniquet to staunch the flow of blood from the man's forearm? Years ago as a high school girl she'd taken a course in first aid but—could she remember, now? For a tourniquet you had to use a stick? Her eyes darted about, searching for—what? So slowly she was thinking, with the effort of one trying to walk through sludge in a dream. Like a foolish trapped bird her heart beat erratically in her chest.

The man was insisting he was all right, he could walk to the ranger's station—"Hey, I'm not going to die."

Grotesquely, he tried to laugh. He had no idea how torn and bloody his face was.

The woman helped the man to his feet. How heavy he was, and how uncoordinated! His face was a mask of blood, it was terrifying to see flaps of loose skin in his cheeks and forehead. One of the man's ear lobes had been torn.

At least, the man's eyes had been spared.

The woman gripped the man around the waist, clumsily. With effort he was able to walk leaning heavily on her. The woman was trying to comfort him—she had no idea what she was saying except that there would be help for him soon, he would be all right…She saw that the front and sleeves of her sweater were soaked in dark blood.

By this time the sun had sunk below the tree line. It was now dusk and the air was cold and wet as if after a rain. The woman's teeth were chattering. The woman and the man made their stumbling way along the trail. They'd begun to hear calls, cries—two rangers were running up the shadowy trail with flashlights, shouting. The man was limping, wincing with pain. His clothes had been torn as if with a giant scissors. Though he must have weighed sixty pounds more than she did, the woman was managing to hold him erect, trembling with the effort. As she was about to collapse the man was lifted from the woman's grip.

They were taken to the rangers' station and treated with first aid. Sterilizing liquid, bandages. For the man's lacerated forearm, a tourniquet deftly applied by the elder of the rangers. It was observed that the man was lucky—"The artery wasn't severed." A dog attack was a serious injury, there was the possibility of rabies. It was imperative to locate the dog.

The straggly-bearded young man had fled the park with the mastiff. Incredibly, he had not reported the attack. But others had seen him, and had reported him. A hiker returning to his car in the parking lot had taken down the plate number of the young man's Jeep.

Beneath the bandages, the man's face was ashen. His breath came quickly and shallowly. He was urged to lie down on a cot. Despite his protests, an ambulance was called. Dog bites are highly dangerous, the ranger said. A vicious dog-biting has to be reported. The dog's owner would be prosecuted. And leaving the scene of the attack—the son of a bitch would be charged for that, too.

The man's facial injuries required stitches, that was clear. First aid wouldn't be enough. The woman had seen with horror what the dog's teeth and nails had done to her friend. Already the gauze bandages on his face were darkening with blood.

Within minutes the ambulance arrived in the now near-deserted park. The tearful woman wanted to ride with the injured man in the ambulance but the man insisted that she take his station wagon, and meet him at the hospital; he didn't want his vehicle locked in the park overnight.

Even with his injuries, half-dazed by the attack and speaking with difficulty, the man appeared to be thinking calmly, rationally.

The woman took his key from the man's shaky fingers, and his wallet and backpack, and followed in his station wagon. Followed the ambulance along curving mountain roads. She could not breathe, the loneliness was palpable and suffocating as cotton batting.

Inside the man's station wagon, and the man not at the steering wheel! This seemed unnatural to her, baffling.

She thought *He will be all right. We will be all right, then.*

She could leave him, then. She would call a taxi, and be driven to her home approximately twelve miles away.

Yet it was shocking to her, she could not quite fathom it, the dog's young master had fled the park without reporting the attack. The straggly-bearded young man who'd seemed so concerned about them had cared so little about their welfare, he'd fled knowing that, if his dog wasn't located by authorities, both bite-victims would have to endure rabies shots.

She'd been told by the park rangers that the dog's owner would be apprehended within a few hours. The attack had already been reported to local police. A warrant would be issued for the dog owner's arrest. She'd been assured that authorities would find the man and examine the dog for rabies but in her distressed state she'd scarcely been able to listen, or to care.

At the brightly lighted medical clinic, the woman hurried inside. She understood that she was wild-eyed, splotched with blood, looking distraught and disoriented. She saw—the man was being carried into the ER on a stretcher. To her horror she saw that the man seemed to be only partly-conscious. He didn't seem aware of his surroundings. She asked one of the medical workers what was wrong and was told that her companion had had a kind of "seizure" in the ambulance, he'd lost consciousness, his blood pressure had risen alarmingly and his heartbeat had accelerated, in fibrillation.

Fibrillation! The woman knew only vaguely what this meant.

"Oh God save him," the woman begged. "Don't let him die!"

She was prevented from following the man into the ER. She found herself standing at a counter, being asked questions. Her face was streaked coarsely with tears like a billboard ravaged by weather and rain. She fumbled with the man's wallet, searching for his medical insurance card. His University ID. How slowly she moved, her bandaged hands were clumsy as if she wore mittens. One of the EMT's who'd brought the man into the ER was telling her that she should be treated as well, her lacerated hands and wrists should be examined in the ER, the rangers' first aid wasn't enough. But the woman refused to listen. She had more important matters with which to deal. She flushed with indignation when the woman at the counter asked what relation she was to the injured man and sharply she said:

"I am his fiancée."

~

How long she remained in the ER waiting room the woman would have no clear idea afterward. Time had become disjointed, confusing. Her eyelids were so heavy, she couldn't keep them open. Yet she was sure she hadn't slept for even a few seconds.

Several times she inquired after the man and was told that he was undergoing emergency treatment for cardiac arrhythmia and she could not see him just yet. This news seemed terrible to her, unacceptable. He'd only been bitten by the damned dog! He had not seemed so badly injured initially, he'd insisted upon walking...The woman was light-headed, breathing quickly. Her bandaged hands and wrists throbbed with pain. She heard her thin plaintive voice begging—"Don't let him die!"

With her affrighted eyes she saw how others regarded her. A woman slightly crazed with worry, mounting fear. A woman with a voice raised in panic. A woman of the sort you pity even as you inch away from her.

The woman's clothes were damp with blood. Her blood, and his.

She saw that her coarse-knit sweater, that had been one of her very best, most beautiful and most expensive Scottish sweaters, had been torn and mangled by the massive dog past repair.

On the trail coming down from Wild Cat Canyon Peak she'd been so cold her fingers had stiffened but now her fingers burned and stung beneath the bandages. In a bright fluorescent-lit restroom outside the ER unit her face in the mirror above the sink was blurred like those faces on TV that dissolve into pixels to disguise the guilt of identity. She was thinking of the way in which the massive dog had thrown itself at her and the way, astonishingly, in which the man had protected her from the dog. Her brain felt as if it were throbbing, flailing to comprehend. Did the man love her, then? Or—was she meant to love him? What a coward she'd been, the craven way in which she'd ducked behind the man to save herself, desperately she'd grabbed at him, as she'd have grabbed at anyone, cringing, crouching, whimpering like a terrified child. The man had thrust himself forward to be attacked in her place. A man who was virtually a stranger to her had risked his life for *her*.

Now the woman found herself in possession of the man's wallet. She had his backpack containing his camera equipment. In her state of nervous dread she looked through the wallet which was a leather wallet of good quality but badly worn. Credit cards, university ID, library card. Driver's license. A miniature photo of a tensely smiling middle-aged man with a furrowed forehead and thinning shoulder-length hair whom she would have claimed she'd never seen before. And she discovered that he'd been born in 1956—he was fifty-seven years old! A decade older than she'd have guessed, and sixteen years older than she was.

Another card indicated that the man had a cardiac condition—*mitral valve prolapse*. A much-folded prescription dated several years before for a medication to be administered intravenously. Nearest of kin to be notified in case of emergency, a woman with the man's last name, possibly a sister, who lived in San Diego.

The woman hurried to the ER, to speak with a nurse. She pressed the prescription onto the woman who promised her, yes she'd report this discovery to the cardiac specialist who was overseeing the man's treatment.

They would only humor her, the woman supposed. The hysterical fiancée! They'd performed their own tests upon the stricken man.

"Ma'am?"—the waiting room was nearly empty when an attendant came to inform her that her companion was hospitalized for the night, for further tests in the morning and observation in the cardiac unit. The cardiologist on call had managed to control the man's fibrillation and his heartbeat was near-normal but his blood pressure was still high and his "white blood count" was low. The woman tried to feel a rush of relief. Tried to think *Now I can go home, the danger is past.*

Instead she went upstairs to the third-floor cardiac unit. For several minutes she stood outside the doorway of room 3112 undecided whether to enter. Inside, in a twilit room, the man lay in a bed, unnaturally still, as nurses fussed about him. His heartbeat was monitored by a machine. His breathing was monitored. The woman saw that the first-aid bandages hurriedly applied to his face had been removed, his numerous wounds had been stitched together and bandaged again, in a yet more elaborate and more lurid mask of criss-crossing strips of white. The man's arms and hands had been bandaged as well.

The horror was, the ugly dog had wanted to tear out the man's throat. Tear off his face. And how easily that might have happened.

A kindly beautiful face the woman thought it.

She'd entered the hospital room, her knees were weak with exhaustion. Almost she felt that she might faint. A sick, sinking sensation rose in her bowels, into her chest, a dread beyond nausea. Yet she felt gratitude for the man's courage, and for his kindness. Shame for herself, that she'd valued the man so negligently.

In the room, the woman pulled over a chair and sat beside the man's bed. Slowly the woman moved like a person in a dream not her own.

The man had been undressed, his torn and bloodied clothes removed from him. In a hospital gown he lay unnaturally still, eyes shut. His breathing was quick and shallow but rhythmic. The bed had been cranked at a thirty-three-degree angle to allow for easier breathing.

His eyelids fluttered, startled. Was he seeing her? Did he recognize her? The tear-ravaged face. The bandaged hands and wrists. The woman thought *He has forgotten my name.*

From what the woman could make out of his stitched-together face beneath the bandages, the man was trying to speak. Or—trying to smile?

He was asking her—what? She tried to understand but his words were slurred.

The woman reached over, to take the man's hand. His fingers too were bandaged, and felt cold, stiff. She squeezed his fingers, and the man squeezed back.

She heard herself explain that she would be staying for a while. Until visiting hours ended. She had his wallet and his camera and the key to his station wagon and other things of his, for safekeeping.

She said she would return in the morning, when he was to be discharged. She would drive him home, then. If he wanted. If he needed her. She would return, and bring his things with her, and drive him home. Did he understand?

In the cranked-up bed, the man drifted into sleep. They'd given him a sedative, the woman supposed. Powerful medication to calm his racing heart.

His mouth eased open, he breathed heavily, wetly. This was the night-breathing the woman recalled, and felt comforted to hear. The woman practiced pronouncing his name: "Simon." This seemed to her a beautiful name. A name new to her, in her life, for she'd before never known anyone named Simon.

Now they were safe, tears spilled from the woman's eyes, and ran in rivulets down her ravaged face. She was crying as she had not cried in memory. She was too old for such emotion, there was something ridiculous and demeaning about it. Yet, she was remembering how at the top of the steep trail the man had insisted that she drink from his plastic water bottle. She hadn't wanted to drink the lukewarm water, yet had drunk it as the man watched, acquiescing, yet with resistance, resentment. In their relationship the man would be the stronger, the woman would resent the man's superior strength, yet she would be protected by it. She might defy it, but she would not oppose it. She was thinking of the two or three occasions when she'd kissed the man in a pretense of an emotion she hadn't yet felt.

Like the man, the woman was exhausted. She continued to hold the man's hand on the outside of the covers, less tightly now. She lay her head against the headrest of the chair beside the bed. Her heavy eyelids closed. Vividly she saw the man at the peak of Wild Cat Canyon trail, holding his heavy camera aloft, peering through the viewing lens. A chill wind stirred his thinning silvery-coppery hair—she hadn't noticed that before. She must hurry to him, she must stand close beside him. She must slide her arm around his waist, to steady him. This was her task, her duty. He was stronger than she, but a man's strength can drain from him. A man's courage can be torn from him, and bleed away. She was terrified of something, was she? The pale-blue rim of the Pacific Ocean, far away at the horizon. The bald-sculpted hills and exquisite little lakes that seemed unreal as papier-mâché you could poke your fingers through. And to her horror she realized she'd been hearing a heavy panting breath, a chuffing-wet breath, somewhere behind them, and below them on the trail, in the gathering dusk, waiting.

TWO POEMS

JOYCE CAROL OATES

THE TUNNEL

Early April, descending
the long broken hill
behind Panoramic Way.

Morning radioactive-bright.
The hill a puzzle of concrete outcroppings
broken and discontinuous as the aphorisms of Nietzsche.

And the Tunnel not (yet) visible
though its peristalsis begins
to pull, squeeze, tug.

In the dazzling distance,
San Francisco Bay.
As you descend the hill

the glittering Bay retreats
like a memory of happiness
but still

the palette is wide, seemingly random
in sunshine like spangled coins
the curious uneven descent

like a drunk
staggering
and the Tunnel not (yet)

defined as in a canvas
of Magritte where it's the absence of
depth that assures

This is art, not life.
This will not hurt you.

And now passing
the abandoned house
gigantic, stucco

strangely surrounded by chain-link fencing,
razor wire absurd in swagger
protecting what no one wants.
And still you descend the hill
bravely, boldly
blindly seeing now

the deserted playing field,
deserted playground.
Stilled swings, rusted slide

O where has life gone?—
abandoning these places
abruptly at Warring Street,

and then to Derby
more rapidly now
the Tunnel narrows

at Stuart, College, Russell too
swiftly passing way-stations
of ordinary life

you would clutch at, in
your descent
except sucked by peristalsis

tugged past, breathless
and now the sky lowered
like a sound-proofed ceiling

unremitting, no mercy
at Ashby Avenue
rudely tugged as a teat

made to turn right onto Ashby,
as the morning shudders
visibly, you can feel shrinkage

as out of pastel treetops
the Hospital emerges
grim in efficiency

the "boundless" sky
has vanished, at the Hospital
driveway in the grip

of peristalsis tugged
through the automatic doors
in whose glass a frightened face

appears, disappears
and into the twilit foyer
and to the double elevators

rising inexorably to the sixth floor
to room 765
where your life awaits you

sleeping, a tube in his bruised nose
clasped hands on the distended belly
breathing in random gusts

like the lone wind at shore,
and a sickle moon above.

O Love—where will you abide when our frail bodies are no more?

PALLIATIVE

1.

Hate hope!
Arsenic for weeks
we'd taken in micro-drops
on credulous tongues.

Hope the thing
with noisome wings
clattering
about our heads
with a broom at last swatted to earth.
Stomped, smashed.

Now, clarity of silence.
Only the drip of minimal liquids—saline, Dilaudin.
Only the labored and arrhythmic breathing
as the chest rises, falls—rises,
falls.
Faintest of echoes—*Give up on.*

2.

Hold desperation
like a playing card
close to the heart
reluctant to reveal
what you feel
but (yes) you risk
the irrevocable loss
too late.

And so on the brink of *too late*
(when no one else is in the room)
(for a hospice room can be crowded)
(by "crowded" meaning more than two people)
you tell your husband that you love him
so much, what a wonderful
husband he has been
and he says—*But I failed you by dying.*
And you protest—*But why are you saying
such a thing, you are not
dying, we are talking
Here together!*—
And he says *Because I am dead.*

As after the final biopsy
he'd been incensed—*They took my soul from me.
They took me to the crematorium, I saw the sign.
Don't try to tell me I didn't see the sign.*

3.
*Trapped in this bed like a prison.
Is the car out front? Drive the car around.
Where are the keys to the car?
Joyce, don't leave. Joyce?
We need to get the car. Where are the keys...
I want to go home. Take me home. Joyce—
don't leave me!
What did we do with the car?*

4.
In hospice time ceases.
Hours lapse into days
and days into night
and again day, and
night and the mouth
once fierce in kissing
and being kissed

is slack, mute.
And breathing slows,
asymmetrical
as a listing boat.
And fever dreams rage
beneath bluish eyelids
quivering in secret life.
Until at last the deepest sigh
of a lifetime…

5.
After such struggle
you must love
the unrippled dark
water in which
the perfect cold O
of the moon floats

FOUR POEMS

NOAH WARREN

CUT LILIES

More than a hundred dollars of them.

It was pure folly. I had to find more glass things to stuff them in.

Now a white and purple cloud is breathing in each corner

of the room I love. Now a mass of flowers spills down my dining table—

each fresh-faced, extending its delicately veined leaves

into the crush. Didn't I watch

children shuffle strictly in line, cradle

candles that dribbled hot white on their fingers,

chanting Latin—just to fashion Sevilla's Easter? Wasn't I sad? Didn't
I used to

go mucking through streambeds with the skunk cabbage raising

bursting violet spears?—Look, the afternoon dies

as night begins in the heart of the lilies and smokes up

their fluted throats until it fills the room

and my lights have to be not switched on.

And in close darkness the aroma grows so sweet,

so strong, that it could slit me. It does.

I know I'm not the only one whose life is a conditional clause hanging from something to do with spring and one tall room and the tremble of my phone.

I'm not the only one that love makes feel like a dozen

flapping bedsheets being ripped to prayer flags by the wind.

When I stand in full sun I feel I have been falling headfirst for decades.

God, I am so transparent.

So light.

IF WE ARE TO GO FORWARD

Don't let your shoulders wilt as you sit at the table
sinking your head into the flowers
you snipped and fed.

Don't cry because you wound up in this room
as this fragile little person. Even you
saw, or heard, or sensed
moments of choice
walking past.

Don't cry, not even silently. If the wetness
should rot the lilies' smooth faces
so soon, if they should shut
and bloom inward again,
where would you turn?

Or if like a herd they should sense your breath
among them, if they should begin to quiver
and circle, and glow, faint at first
then unbearable, twenty
wan suns flaring

Absurdly in the gloom above you, all around you, no matter
where you turn in the frigid wood,
your slender heart thrashing,
your eyes dead in the glare,
then who, then what
have you become?

AUTOMATIC POOL CLEANER

Like the stubborn rover *Spirit* it's
insistent in collecting its units
of grime, if less scientific. Like a white ray
it cruises slowly through teal.
It's someone's leashed flounder, or
a menace that has come too close
to the surface and now spurts
from his tail a warm cupful
that misses my leather sandals.

Look at him go. Ingeniously
independent, he's replaced
the pool boy, whose dim ghost
imbues him with comic eros
and just a nibble of pathos.

But as he tries to force a way
into the shallows, where scalloped steps
march down—rise up—
he becomes bewildered. His flagellum
lashes sadly forth and back.
I haul him up and turn
him toward the deeper center.

Faithful as a Labrador
he scoots away on his errand
and his wake laps my ankles:
isn't everything real entirely real?
Plastic shoes, plastic chair, so what;

I too have been known
to ceaselessly pace a little cell.

The lawn, fertilized, gasps
weakly in the dense heat as it grows.
Yellow as cake, an inner tube
drifts over the snarl
of the machine's umbilical.

It's Tuesday at three. Friends of mine
are off in offices, classrooms, labs, Brazil,
or the Bay creating wealth,
girding for a future they pursue.

But their acquaintance sips icy coffee
in his latest attempt to fire
his forebrain to a lyre: some thing
he can hold and have, that returns
more life than it burns, a thing
gorgeous, worthless, and self-betraying.

O sun on water, O sun on matter.
Kiss my limbs, my lips as I recline away
into this, the prime of my decay.

ACROSS FROM THE WINTER PALACE

Do you remember when you began to travel?
It lent you this astonishing lens and you kept a journal
That rode in your breast pocket like a stone.
There you wrote "Limoges—" and "Altenkirchen"
And when you kissed, saw a *peasant*, or passed out—
Died for twenty seconds—in the heat on the hill above
Marseille you would rush out the notebook and make a note—
Sometimes just an x in the top right corner—
And ideally you would brood about that later.

Which led slowly to the dark hot bar
Where you enjoy a glass of beer across from the Winter Palace in summer.
In the rose-and-blue windows of the basilica
Today radiant burghers stood and learned Mercy in a circle
Around Stephen, recognized
By the pebble enthroned in his skull and the scarlet ooze.

While in your system the amphetamines progress.
The idea is they'll give you heart to haul yourself up and cross
The limestone plaza. And when at the gate of the place
You pay you can enter the Palace.

EARLY MORNING THOUGHTS ON AHAB

PETER ORNER

Last night, deep into *Moby Dick*, on page 667, I was surprised when Ishmael announces, out of nowhere, that not very long before the Pequod set sail, Ahab was found, writhing in pain, on a cobblestone street in Nantucket after his ivory leg have out from under him and stabbed him in the groin. This incident is, to my knowledge, the single glimpse in the entire novel of Ahab on land. Where was he coming from? Where was he going? Ishmael doesn't seem to know. Nor does he tell us how he knows this story or who even he heard it from. But Ishmael does say, curiously, that Ahab was found and assisted by "someone unknown."

Now here's a character who has long since transcended the book he was written into, who's known by millions of people who have never cracked open the novel as that lunatic captain Ahab. And yet look at him now, sprawled in the street, helpless, and a stranger comes to him, hoists him up—touches him. This strikes me. That this someone unknown would have had to touch Ahab's body in order to help him. And presumably, Ahab allowed this person to do so.

Ishmael claims, again without offering any evidence, that the accident so scarred Ahab that it explains why he remained locked in his cabin during the key first few days of the voyage, seen by nobody. At that time, hundreds of pages earlier in the book, Ishmael had remarked that he was nervous about Ahab's absence from the deck, because a sailor likes to have a look at his captain before entrusting the man with his life for three years sailing oceans.

But by that time the Pequod was already underway, so what choice did he have? When we do finally glimpse Ahab for the first time—he makes a sudden appearance in deck days into the voyage—Ishmael remarks that he looks like a man who's just been cut away from a burning stake.

And here, today, comes Ishmael's assertion, again, hundreds of pages that Ahab's demented state of mind stems as much, if not more, from the fact that he'd once fallen down on a dark street as the white whale's munching his leg off in the first place.

This all got me thinking this morning. I was walking the dog along a cliff by the ocean when I stopped to watch the waves play with some logs as if they were chopsticks. I thought of Ahab and how he called out to a ship called the *Albatross* that was heading home after its own long voyage:

> Ahoy there! This is the Pequod, bound round the world!
> Tell them to address all future letters to the Pacific Ocean! and
> this time three years, if I am not at home, tell them to—

Tell them to what? Ahab never finishes this sentence so we're left to wonder. Send the letters where, Ahab? Where?

I find that lately I do more reading than writing, and more thinking, by far, than either. I read at night until I fall asleep with the light on, some book tented over my nose, and in the morning I wander around the edge of this cliff thinking about what I read the night before. But isn't thinking a form of writing without the pressure of needing to communicate with anybody? I'm testing out the possibility of writing a book in my head and only in my head.

The Israeli novelist Yoel Hoffman once wrote: "It did once indeed occur to this author that he could write a book that is all blank pages."

It is late June 2015; a grotesque month in America is just about over. In Charleston, South Carolina, less than a mile away from where my daughter's grandmother lives, a boy with the same bowl haircut I had as a kid spent an hour listening to a group of people talk about the bible. That night this small group was studying Mark 4, Verses 16 to 20.

> Others, like seed sown on rocky places, hear the word and
> at once receive it with joy. But since they have no root, they last
> only a short time. When trouble or persecution comes because
> of the word, they quickly fall away.

I'm not asking this rhetorically: Did that kid hear a word? A single word? Send those letters where, Ahab?

And this morning as I was walking the dog by the bluff overlooking the Pacific it occurred to me that maybe Ahab was just afraid. Maybe this is all it ever amounted to, ordinary fear. He was afraid to go home, afraid to walk his own streets once again. Afraid, for some reason, to return home to his family, to his own wife and young son. There's a moment it almost happens. Maybe you remember it? Late, very late in the book, just before all hell breaks loose, Starbuck implores Ahab to turn the boat eastward, arguing that it's not too late to change direction and call this whole thing off, that the two of them could still live to see their wives and children again, to return home, yes, home…

Oh, my captain! my captain! noble soul! grand old heart, after all! why should any one give chase to that hated fish! Away with me! let us fly these deadly waters! Let us home. Wife and child, too, are Starbuck's—wife and child of his brotherly, sisterly play-fellow youth; even as thine, Sir, are the wife and child thy loving, paternal old age! Away! let us away!—this instant let me alter the course! How cheerily, how hilariously, O my Captain, would we bowl on our way to see old Nantucket again! I think, Sir, they have some such mild blue days, even as this, in Nantucket.

And by God, it nearly works. Ahab responds:

They have, they have. I have seen them—some summer days in the morning. About this time—yes, it is his noon nap now—the boy vivaciously wakes; sits up in bed; and his mother tells him of me, of cannibal old me; how I am abroad upon the deep, but will yet come back to dance him again.

Of course, if they'd chalked up the hunt for the white whale we wouldn't have a tragedy, and without a tragedy we wouldn't have the book. Plot's got to do what plot has got to do. Some kid doped on hate shows up at a Bible study—

But did you notice something? Ahab, of all people on earth, knows the exact time of day his kid wakes up from his nap. Ahab never will get back to dance that boy again and he knows it. Maybe Ahab concocted the whole insane, murderous ordeal to simply avoiding having to go home. Home? There's no going home. Because there, and only there, existed a nameless terror he couldn't sail onward into the deep and pretend to hunt.

ATITLÁN

PETER ORNER

She'd gone to Guatemala with another guy. I don't know what happened. I didn't ask. She called me collect, crying. I told my boss my grandmother died.

"Another one? What? You've got five grandmothers?"

"My beloved step-grandmother Swenson who raised me from a pup."

"I should have fired your ass fourteen months ago."

"Before I was hired?"

"Get the fuck out of here."

I took a Taca airlines flight to Guatemala City. The entire flight the overhead bin doors flapped like wings. From Guatemala City, I took a yellow school bus to Antigua. Beautiful old colonial town. Buildings, once white, now sooty. She'd been enrolled in a Spanish immersion course. She dropped out after whatever happened with the guy she went down there with. Buenos dias mi vida. She met me at the bus. That was the year she wore a headband. Her arm was in a sling. I didn't ask about that, either. We took another yellow school bus to a smaller town and then took off on foot, our backpacks leaning us forward so that we walked like hunchbacks, to a village at the edge of Lake Atitlán. I still talk to myself about Guatemala. Eighteen years and I write it out on restaurant tables with my finger. I once read that Debussy used to play songs on the closed piano lid.

~

We took a room in a one room inn run by a stooped, crippled Pole. He spoke with a British accent he said he picked up during the war. He told us he flew for the RAF until the Nazis shot him down over France.

Military pension. Washed up in Guatemala in the early sixties and never left. He discoursed in that sing-song English about homemade wine and death squads. He said once in a while the natives need to be reminded that they're natives. "Though I must emphasize that, of course—" One tap of his cane. Another tap of his cane. "—that on a personal level I quite detest killing."

In the afternoons a little girl brought us coffee to a table on the edge of the shore. She was lanky, eyes like full moons. She curtseyed while still balancing the tray atop one palm. Eyed each of us a moment before setting the coffees down and backing away. When the tide came in, it washed over the legs of the table.

Our room looked out upon the lake and in the morning, out of the midst, the cone of the volcano rose up out of the water.

At night, it rained. I'd go out and stand on the beach in the still sun-heated rain.

∼

Toward dawn on the last night I woke up and she was sitting on the edge of the bed, wearing only a t-shirt and her headband.

"You can't sleep?"

"It doesn't matter."

"Is it Mike?"

"Who's Mike?"

"The guy from Spanish immersion."

"Chris."

"So, Chris?"

"What about him?"

"What happened to your arm?"

"You think Mike beat me up?"

"Chris—"

"I tripped on a hole running in Antigua. Good health care. I didn't pay a thing."

She leaned back and spoke to the ceiling fan whose blades rotated slowly above us like we were in an Antonioni movie. She spoke, if I remember, for a long time to the ceiling fan. Life and death and sweat— we couldn't take off enough those nights—and I can't remember a single thing she said. About me she once said that I could never see the forest through the trees. It's a phrase I still don't understand. Aren't the trees the forest? I remember the day we met and I rode home no-handed through the Presidio Cemetery and sang to the graves. Insane to be that happy, get you arrested by the park police—

We used to play a game where we'd pretend we'd just met.

"I'm Harv. Sorry, I didn't catch your—"

"Diane Somerville. Human Resources."

"Terrific to meet you, Diane. What brings you to the office party, the office party?"

"Look, I got to go feed my cats."

She's in Seattle now. A political scientist, which to me is a hilarious job title. Sometimes I call her.

"Hello?"

I pant a little into the phone.

"Harv? Harv Nadelson?"

"In the flesh."

"You're naked?"

"Sure."

"Gross. Fat now?"

"Getting there."

"Nice, fat guys are in. Chubby dads—"

"What happened with that guy?"

"Which one?"

"Spanish immersion."

"Oh, Atitlán, the volcano. You were a hero, Harv. You saved me. Is that what you want to hear?"

"Yes."

"How are you?"

"I don't know."

~

The old Pole said he wouldn't go back to Europe in a box. He said if nobody murdered you Guatemala was glorious.

THE MERE WIFE

AN EXCERPT

MARIA DAHVANA HEADLEY

Prologue

Say it. The beginning and end at once. I'm facedown in a truck bed, getting ready to be dead. I think about praying, but I've never been any good at asking for help. I try to sing. There aren't any songs for this. All I have is a line I read in a library book. *All shall be well and all shall be well and all manner of thing shall be well.*

There's a sack over my head, but I'm seeing the faces of dead soldiers. I'm watching the war in slow motion, and then too fast, a string of men, a line of blood and baffled eyes—

We got lost. All of us got sent to the wrong country, and everyone but me is dead. Now I think all countries are the wrong country, and I'm out here, two minutes from gone.

My guys are ghosts, and my girls too. My best friend Renee got killed a week ago, slipped on a step, made a noise, and bullets, fast as wasps. I had her in my arms when she died. Three days ago, I was riding in a truck with Lynn Graven from Gulfport, who told me the Mississippi River had wandered according to its own hungers, changed its path in order to drink up land it wanted to claim, and then told me that there was a river like that in this desert too, and we should swim in it and see if it drank us. He dove out of the truck we were in at eighty miles per hour, thinking he'd land in water. Raul Honrez grew up in Idaho, his parents fruit pickers. He got halfway through med school before the planes flew into the towers and he joined up. I watched his body blow apart, right before someone grabbed me and threw me into this truck.

Two months ago I was on leave, far away from all this.

"*Listen!*" Someone shouted from the sidewalk, and she held on to my ankle. She had a sign that read YES. I GOT LOST. ANYTHING HELPS. She'd come from the same war I'd come from. Tin dish, rattling for change.

"Listen, lemme tell you what's gonna come for you," she said. "Gimme five bucks."

"You can have everything," I told her, and dropped the contents of my wallet into her dish.

"Then I'll tell you everything I know," she said.

"No, thanks," I said, and walked.

"You're gonna live forever!" she shouted after me. "You're the one who gets away! You're gonna lose some shit, though, so you better watch out."

"I don't have anything to lose," I said to her, cocky for no reason.

You go into war knowing you're signing up to be a goner. Living is luck, not anything special. You're not magic. You're just lucky.

I figured I knew the shape of things. I'd been fighting a while. I signed up right after people stopped volunteering, in the middle of a war that went on forever. They made me think it was about heroes. That's how they sell it to you when you're seventeen. Go out and save the starving, the war-torn, the children, and the women. Instead, you march in and roll down roads, close your eyes and shoot. Hungry people on rations, scared people, fucked-up people, shooting by clothes and color of skin, or by the way bodies send out heat. Bright blots on a map, hearts beating.

I figured I'd been lucky so far. I figured that if I died, I died.

I got on a plane and came back to the desert.

Now I'm rattling down the road, and there's nowhere I want to go, no good option. If I'm being taken, I'm going into a prison, or I'm going up on a screen. My brain's shaking up old things, distractions, picking over the moments leading me here, grabbing things I should have paid attention to when people said them.

"*Listen!*" an old woman said to me ten years ago, on a Greyhound Bus. "Let me tell you a story!"

I was seventeen and didn't know that I could move away, so I listened. Windows full of places. Night and the highway, lights green and red, people in every car going somewhere, and beside me this woman, telling me her version of the story of the world, all the things that ever happened from the beginning of time to the end of it. Thirty hours.

"This is the thing about history," she said. "People lie about the parts they missed. They tell you they know what happened, the world exploded and they watched it, when really all they did was hear a sound so loud it shook the ground. You never understand the whole story until you're at the end of it. If you're the last one standing, you're the one who sings for everyone else's funeral. But at least you get to be the one who tells it. You tell it for the rest of us."

I looked at her, sitting next to me, her shaky hands and church hat. She looked old enough to have been born in the single digits.

I thought I knew everything.

I thought I knew what the Earth had in it. I thought I knew what was coming for me. Now I know all this was waiting for me, this desert, this sack, this stumble as they drag me out of the truck.

I hear the whetting of a blade.

I don't know who they are, whoever has me, but I'm their *them*, and they're mine. We are each other's nightmares. I'm on my knees in the sand. They give me words, and I say them for the video.

"My name is Dana Mills," I say. "America, this is your doing."

I feel the wind of the blade swinging back, and I'm in a thousand cities at once, *all shall be well*, and in a thousand countries, and I'm on a ship coming across an ocean, *and all shall be well*, and I'm an old woman dying on a mountain, the last of my family, the last of my line, *and all manner of thing shall be well*, and there's blackness, and in the blackness, there's a bright star, and it gets bigger, and bigger—

"Listen," someone whispers into my ear. "Listen to me."

Am I dead?

"Listen," the voice whispers. "In some countries, you kill a monster when it's born. Other places, you kill it only when it kills someone else. Other places, you let it go, out into the forest or the sea, and it lives there forever, calling for others of its kind. Listen to me, it cries. Maybe it's just alone."

I wake up, gasping, underneath sand. Grit between my fingertips. There's space around my face, but nowhere else. I feel my heart beating, though, and that tells me something.

The sand is heavy and hot. Sunlight through my eyelids. I move sand with my fingertips, then with my whole body, until my hand comes out into the air. I push myself out, and stand up, swaying. There's an unfamiliar weight, and I look down at my stomach.

I'm a tent in the middle of the desert, and someone's inside it, someone who doesn't speak and doesn't march, who just sleeps. I almost laugh. I almost cry. I don't know who the father is.

I'm the mother.

This is how I come back from the dead. Six months pregnant. This is what I have. This is what I own.

I look out across the sand, and there's movement at the edge of it, ripples of heat, silhouettes of people moving. I start walking.

Hours in, something blows up ten feet from me. A shard of shrapnel in my eye, blood running down my cheek, nothing else. I tie my shirt around my face and keep going.

I walk until I get to Americans. I look so bad no one knows which side I'm on. They freak out when they get close. They read my tags.

Shitfuck, it's Dana Mills. Get someone.

I wake up later, under lights, shaved all over, my head, my pubic hair, my legs, my armpits, like someone on her way to be cooked. There are bars on the windows. There's a patch over my eye, and I feel drugged.

"Tough luck," says the girl in the bed beside mine. She doesn't have legs. "Guess it's too late now," she says. "For all of us stupid fuckers."

"Guess it is."

"I made it out of where I came from and I'm never going back," she says. "I got no one out there in the whole wide world."

"Me neither," I say. "My mother's dead. I'm alone."

We both look at my stomach.

"You're not," she says. "You got that one. Whoever that one's gonna be."

She has freckled skin and a pointed nose, crooked lips covered in black lipstick like she's planning to go to a club and throw herself into a mosh pit. Maybe she's eighteen, the same age I was when I joined up. Her fingernails are longer than regulation and polished with glitter. I don't ask her what she did. She doesn't ask me.

"So, are you crazy?" she asks, without fanfare. "*I* am. I see things. Mostly I see my legs. Why am I alive, anyway? Is that what you're thinking? That's what I'm thinking."

I'm in the middle of replying when I see something light up in the center of her chest. A flicker. A flame?

"What's in there?" I ask, but she's gone.

Five men are in her place, making themselves at home, feet on the bedframe, one or two looming over me, looking at my charts. Letting me know I'm the only one in the room who can't run. Being barefoot, once you've been to war, is terrifying.

"What happened to you, soldier? Who took you?"

"I don't know," I say. I'm still looking for the girl, but there's no girl.

A guy kneels in front of me, looking at me with all sincerity, like I can't tell him from a good person.

"We saw you on television," the man says. "You were lucky. You were still pretty enough for video. The rest of your team got blown up."

I think about luck.

"We watched you die. It was convincing."

"But I'm alive," I say. My skin's prickling all over.

"Execution by edit." He gestures at my stomach. "Whose child is this?"

"Mine." I don't expect to say that, but it's what I say.

"Rape? Or consensual?"

One answer means I'm a victim, and the other means I'm a collaborator, and I don't know, so I don't answer. I hear one of them say something about DNA tests. My brain is skipping like a record. They hypnotize me, insist I tell them everything. There's nothing to tell, except that I'm back from wherever I've been, that I'm alive, and that I'm pregnant.

I stay in the hospital that isn't a hospital for six weeks and then I feel my baby under my ribs, kicking hard.

There are other soldiers working in the prison. I find a guy who was stationed where I was. He gets me out in the middle of the night, a key in my food, a map under my plate, and I run. When I can't find a train, I hide myself in trailers carrying horses. Go under a tarp in the back of a pickup. Wake up in a parking lot one night with someone staring at me, punch him in the side of the head, and take off into the dark.

I see the girl from the hospital again in a truck stop bathroom. She walks out of a stall without the use of legs and says, "Hey," and I say *hey* back to her like I'm not worried about my sanity. Her fingers are nothing but skeleton. She's smoking a cigarette.

In the center of her chest there's an open wound, and through it I can see her ribs, her lungs, a candle lit, balanced on her solar plexus and surrounded by gilding.

"God get to you yet? God ask for any favors?" she asks.

"I don't know," I say. "Something happened to me. I don't know what. I don't know what's happening to me now, either."

"Something happened to me too. God got me, and now I'm dead," she says. "I started spitting fire, and then I turned to ice and melted and everyone around me said I was a martyr. I got painted by every painter. You've seen me on walls and on drugstore candles. Go get one if you want." She indicates the votive in her chest. "Might help you."

The girl takes a long drag, and her cheeks suck in so far I can see what her skull looks like.

"Still hurts," she says. "You don't want to go this way, even if you get famous. Your face shows up on burnt toast and you never stop feeling like you can't get a good breath. Still, it's better than the alternative."

"What's the alternative?" I ask.

"Oh," she says. "You know. Eternal flame."

She walks out of the bathroom, legless, leaving footprints made of fire, but then they're gone and I'm standing there, one hand wrapped in paper.

My baby kicks inside me, cars pull in and out of the lot, trucks make that grieving moan of too heavy and brakes half broken. I see a bunch of them pull off the highway and uphill because nothing works on a big thing, nothing but gravity.

I keep going. Why am I going home at all? It occurs to me that they'll know where I came from, and be waiting for me. But they aren't. Nobody's there.

I guess that's because where I came from is gone.

I'm having contractions, close enough together that I'm scared, and all that's left in the place where I used to live is a bright white light, a fence around new buildings, and a mountain.

Every life starts with the same beginning and ends with the same end. The rest is the story, even if you don't understand it, if even if you aren't sure which parts are true and which parts are your brain trying to make sense out of smoke. I grew up in a house looking up at this mountain. I left this place forever, but forever is over. Now I'm back here again.

I climb, stumbling up the slope, through the trees and toward the cave.

Listen, I think. Listen.

Part I

The Mountain

Listen. Long after the end of everything is supposed to have occurred, long after apocalypses have been calculated by cults and calendared by computers, long after the world has ceased believing in miracles, there's a baby born inside a mountain.

Earth's a thieved place. Everything living needs somewhere to be.

There's a howl and then a whistle, and then a roar. Wind shrieks around the tops of trees, and sun melts the glacier at the top of the peak. Even stars sing. Boulders avalanche and snow drifts, ice moans.

No one needs to see us for us to exist. No one needs to love us for us to exist. The sky is filled with light.

The world is full of wonders.

We're the wilderness, the hidden river, and the stone caves. We're the snakes and songbirds, the storm water, the brightness beneath the darkest pools. We're an old thing made of everything else, and we've been waiting here a long time.

We rose up from an inland sea, and now, half beneath the mountain, half outside it, is the last of that sea, a mere. In our soil there are tree fossils, the remains of a forest, dating from the greening of the world. They used to be a canopy; now they spread their stone fingers underground. Deep inside the mountain, there's a cave full of old bones. There was once a tremendous skeleton here, rib cage curving the wall, tail twisting across the floor.

Later, the cave was widened and pushed, tiled, tracked, and beamed to house a train station. The bones were pried out and taken to a museum, reassembled into a hanging body.

The station was a showpiece before it wasn't. The train it housed went back and forth to the city, cocktail cars, leather seats. The cave's walls are crumbling now, and on top of the stone the tiles are cracking, but the station remains: ticket booth, wooden benches, newspaper racks, china teacups, stained-glass windows facing outward into earthworms, and crystal chandeliers draped in cobwebs. There are drinking fountains tapping the spring that feeds the mountain, and there's a wishing pool covered in dust.

No train's been through our territory in almost a hundred years. Both sides of the tunnel are covered with metal doors and soil, but the gilded chamber remains, water pouring over the tracks. Fish swim in the rail river and creatures move up and down over the mosaics and destination signs.

We wait, and one day our waiting is over.

A panel in the ceiling moves out of position, and a woman drops through the gap at the end of an arch, falling a couple of feet to the floor, panting.

She's bone-thin but for her belly. She staggers, leans against our wall, and looks up at our ceiling, breathing carefully.

There's a blurry streak of light, coming from the old skylight, a portal to the world outside. The world inside consists only of this woman, dressed in stained camo, a tank top, rope-belted fatigues, combat boots, a patch over one eye, hair tied back in a piece of cloth. Her face is scarred with a complicated pink line. On her back, there are two guns and a pack of provisions.

She eases herself down to the tiles. She calls, to any god, to all of them. She calls to us.

Tree roots dangle through the ceiling tiles. A wandering bird swoops down from the outside world, makes its way through the arch, and settles into a secret nest glittered with hoop earrings made of brass, candy wrappers, bits of ribbon.

The woman screams, and her scream echoes from corner to corner of the station, and there is no train, and no help. There is no one but us, silent, and this woman, alone underground. She grits her teeth, and pushes.

We watch. We wait.

The labor takes a day and a night. The sun transits the sky, and the moon slips through the skylight.

The baby latches fingers into the woman's rib cage, toes into her pelvis, and forces itself out breech, unfolding, punching, pressing against something that will not give, and then does.

She screams once more, and then her son is born, wet, small, bloody. He takes his first breath. He gasps, gagging on air, his fingers spread.

His mother's eyes flicker with fire, and her hands glow, as though a bomb has exploded in the far distance, not outside but in.

She breathes. She clenches her fists and brings a knife out of her pack. She cuts the cord and ties it off with a strip of cotton from her shirt. She looks at her child, holding him up into the thin beam of light.

The baby's eyes open, golden, and his mouth opens too. He's born with teeth. His mother looks at him, her face uncertain. She holds him carefully, her hands shaking.

Wonders have been born before. Sometimes they've been worshipped. There've been new things over and over, and some creatures have fallen groaning to the ground and others have learned to fly.

Never mind the loneliness of being on Earth. That will come later.

She touches the baby's face. She washes him with our water, and swaddles him in her shirt, tight against her body.

"Gren," she whispers.

In our history, the history of the mountain, of the land that surged up out of the darkness at the bottom of the sea, this is only an instant, and then it will be dark again.

"Listen," she whispers to the baby.

All the other things that have been born here rise silently in the water of the mere to listen with him, toothed, clawed, each with its own ridge of spiny gleam.

The mountain's citizens look at the infant for a moment, listen to his mother for a moment, and then dive back into the depths.

He is born.

THAT TIME AT MY BROTHER'S WEDDING

LAILA LALAMI

You seem lost, Miss. Are you looking for the American consulate station? I could tell, you see, by your hat and backpack and the documents you hold tight to your chest. It's true that petty theft can be a risk in Casablanca, but I assure you the airport is a secure building. No one will take your papers away. Sit, sit. At a distance, of course, we both know the rules. Make yourself comfortable. It will be a few hours before the consular officers arrive and, even then, it will take them a while to set up their table and start clearing passengers for departure.

How long have I been waiting? A long time, I'm sorry to say. These repatriation flights are for citizens only and—if space allows—residents. But apparently space has not allowed, at least not for the last two weeks. Every time I've put in a request, I've gotten the same answer: "Sorry, Ms. Bensaïd, the flight is full." I thought of trying the airport in Tangier, but train service is closed and in any case there are probably more people waiting there than here. The consular officers keep telling me I should be patient, I will have better luck next time.

The thing is, it was luck that brought me here in March. Ordinarily, I visit my family in the summer, when I am off from teaching, but early this year my brother announced that he was getting married. His fourth time, can you imagine? He scheduled the ceremony smack dab in the middle of my spring break, just to counter what he knew would be my immediate objection. Even so, I told him I couldn't attend because I had plans to go to Texas with my bird-watching group. But he's always had a knack for making me feel guilty. He brought up how thrilled our mother would be to see me, how she's getting on in years, how I should take every chance I get to spend some time her. I couldn't say no to that.

Still, I was disappointed that my plans had been disrupted, so I scheduled a short trip to Merja Zerga, a hundred and forty miles north from here. Have you been? Oh, you'll have to visit someday. It's a tidal lagoon, a Ramsar-designated site in fact, home to an impressive variety of bird species. I wanted to see waders and marsh owls and, with any luck, flamingoes and marbled teals, which migrate through the area this time of year.

Before that, of course, I had to suffer through the wedding. It's not that I don't want to see my brother happy, you understand, it's just that he has terrible taste in women. All of them young, naïve, and in awe of him. At the ceremony—invariably a lavish celebration that saddled his in-laws with debt—he would stand beside his new wife as if he were posing for a fashion magazine. My role was to be the dowdy older sister, completing the family tableau by standing in the background, slightly out of focus.

I had played the part often enough that I arrived at the ceremony ready to take my cues. There were a hundred guests this time, a modest number by my brother's standards, but still enough that it took a long time to make the rounds, being introduced to people and exchanging congratulations and well wishes. The bride's parents were full of questions. "You live in California?" the father asked me.

"Yes," I said. "In Berkeley."

"And what do you teach?"

"Computer science," my mother replied for me. It's a point of pride for her, I think, because initially I had said I wanted to be a painter, which she found impractical.

The father's eyes widened, and there was a murmur as the news traveled to the aunts and uncles and cousins that stood nearby. *California*, someone whispered. *Berkeley*. But the bride was unimpressed; she peered at me with unbounded pity. "How hard it must be for you," she said. Her voice was a squawk. Standing beside her, my brother nodded in agreement.

"What do you mean?" I asked.

"Living so far away."

"Living anywhere can be hard." Wait till you've lived with my dear brother, I thought, and then we'll see who finds life so difficult.

But her attention was already drawn elsewhere. "The photographers are here," she said.

We posed for pictures—the bride and the groom and their families and friends, in different permutations. I started to feel hot flashes coming on, even though I was in a sleeveless gown instead of a heavy caftan. I was rummaging through my purse for my hormone pills when the bride motioned for me to step out of the frame. "Now, let's do one with Moroccans only."

Can you believe it? I was about to say something sharp when my brother intervened. His new wife didn't mean anything bad, he said, it was only that the color of my dress clashed with her caftan. He pulled me back into the frame, beaming his bleach-white smile for the photographers. But I don't think he minded it all that much. Deep down, he resents me because I left home at eighteen while he lives in the house we grew up in, taking care of our mother. Maybe things between us would be different if he'd stayed single like me, instead of flitting from wife to wife every few years.

With all the commotion, I forgot to take my pills. After a few more minutes under the photographers' lights, I got dizzy and tumbled down, catching the bride's train to steady myself. The last thing I heard before I passed out was the flutter of the fabric as it ripped.

The next day, I was preparing for my trip to Merja Zerga, feeling profound thrill at the thought of being on a boat in the lagoon, when I received word that Morocco was closing its borders. I rushed here to try to find a seat on an outbound flight, but no luck so far. Speaking of which, here come the consular officers. I recognize the young man in the blue shirt, he was here two days ago. He's already walking in this direction; he must have noticed the blue passport in your hand. Go on. Perhaps I'll see you on the other side.

SIMPSON WRITING WORKSHOP

NORTHGATE HIGH SCHOOL

NOAH WARREN, SIMPSON FELLOW

POPE FRANCIS PLEASE LET ME GET MARRIED

OLIVIA LOSCAVIO

Pope Francis please let me get married,

I'll go to church every day if you do.

I'm an okay Catholic but I'll be even better if you listen to my proposition for you.

Let me say my vows in the church,

The Cathedral on Polk Street and Pine?

It's where my parents were married, my brother and I christened and it's where my great-grandmother died.

Pope Francis you owe me an apology,

You and God know I can't marry a man.

To me they're like doorknobs or passing cars or sidewalk cracks and to marry one would feel like a sham.

Pope Francis I want to get married,

She's a really good Catholic too.

Far better than me because she still believes despite all that your teachings have put us through.

Pope Francis I'm going to get married,

Hold on to your pointy little hat!

We'd love for you to be there, and understand if you're too busy

But we'd be so happy if you came and said the mass.

Pope Francis I'm finally married,

We had the ceremony just last night.

I stole the keys to the Cathedral and before god and the altar I made that good Catholic my wife.

SAND AND MIRRORS

GRACE DECKER

In a different time, I drove to the ocean for the first time in months, dangling my arm out of the window while taking sharp turns on smooth curves in the road and trying to ignore the weird feeling in my chest I got every time I saw the ocean or a redwood or a poppy swaying in the hills.

I stood for a long time at the shoreline. As dark clouds and patches of sunlight dotted the angry sea, I watched as freezing water surrounded me and burned my legs sinking into the sand. A long time ago someone told me that mirrors were made up of sand, that if you burn it long enough eventually it'll turn into glass, which was hard for me to imagine as murky sand splashed onto my jeans.

If I thought about it, though, it made sense. Everything was made up of something else. Everything was about something else. I had spent so long trying to deny this simple fact, that the things I have tried to forget are still with me, but with the absence of everything I realized that I had devoured and twisted everything that had happened to me until it turned into something else. Something unrecognizable.

See, I loved someone a long time ago who had never tried alcohol and insisted that they never would; they couldn't even stand the sight of it. Someone I thought I hated taught me about all the constellations in the sky and where the names came from. Someone I didn't really know at all once told me that you can only leave so much behind before you're gone too. But I probably shouldn't listen to the last one. That same person told me they were going to bowl in the Olympics.

The thing is now when I get drunk and try not to look up at the sky at night and tell anyone who'll listen that bowling isn't a sport and anyone who thinks so is a fool, I say that it's just my form of rebellion. But I think we all know how that goes.

Because that so-called rebellion just comes down to unspent love in the end. Maybe that's all I'm made up of. Not sand. Unspent love.

Because it's easy to love someone when you know you're never going to see them again. That way the love you had for them is forever immortalized with the person you were and the places you went, no matter how much you might change. You would rather have love kept in hiding places that you have to carry with you than love lost, blurry memories instead of something that might take the love away altogether. Maybe, though, it's much easier to not love at all. But I've never been able to embrace the things that are easy. But that's not the problem.

The problem is that I only know I love something when it's ruined. And now everything is ruined, and I love too much. I love you, and I can never talk about it again. But I think we all know how that goes.

JULY 5TH

DAVID WOOD

A hawk traced the line of Highway One

From the sky before it stretched into the ravine beyond

Our sight, as hours before on this Sunday following the Fourth of July

The roar of contemporary roadsters dipped

And disappeared from the straightaway—then after the sound washed away

Emerged to ascend the grade, a bug-eyed caravan downshifting and spuming exhaust

Into the distant skies. The hawk too breaks from the ravine's shadow.

It dives between the trees, then over the cliffs, undulating on the wind,

Before it returns to a corner rooftop to survey

In silence the ocean below. The constant

Rustle of the waves caresses the cliffs

And seeps into our bedroom undisturbed.

7/6/20

AN ODE TO PRIDE

MICHELLE ALAS

Thoroughly perplexed
am I
by the stigma you
carry
so unwillingly.

As if
you are ugly and
boastful
and not a feeling
of joy
or of success or
even
of prosperity
or of
two happy daughters
who are proud.

Hard workers are proud.
Immigrants are proud.
Single moms are proud
Beautiful people
are proud.
I will carry you with
a head
up high and eyes
ready
to grab every star.

My mother once said
to not
ever duck my head.
My father once said
I could eat the whole
whole world
in one bite if I
wanted.

They are proud of me.
So I
make orgullo
a beautiful word.

I carry
my parents' sacrifice.

IN MY HOUSE

MICHELE ALAS

In my house, our words are melodic. We speak like a song, our speech melting together and a riff punctuating each sentence. I like to think my sing-songy voice is just as harmonious as my parents', but I fear coarse American accents and mispronounced words. At school, all I speak is the hard language of inflection and sharp-edged consonants. At home, my Spanish j's sound like English h's and intonation governs our syntax.

I often find myself overcome by a powerful force known as Spanglish. My brain gets confused and I forget how to say blueberry in Spanish so I say it in English and then my parents correct me and then I feel ashamed. I should know how to say blueberry in Spanish.

The progression is gradual but soon even my sister succumbs to Spanglish. My little sister who was born an American but whose first word was in Spanish. The word was agua. Soon my father succumbs. My father who comes to me when he needs to send an important email in English. I fix his grammar. Soon my mother succumbs. My mother who had lived in this country for fourteen years but would still never get behind the wheel with me when I was learning to drive for fear of an accident. Out of fear of not being understood in an emergency. She sometimes says blueberry instead of arándano. But when we sing and laugh and talk with our families it all sounds like a song.

My father has this funny, vanilla-colored sombrero that he wears to work every day. He says it protects him from the sweltering sun. He beams when he puts it on, the brim of the Panama Hat casting a shadow across his face. My mother laughs, because the hat pinches his head slightly, it is far too small. And she tells him! But he refuses to return it. Their meaningless bickering melts with the whoosh of el viento and the chirps of los pájaros, and another melody forms. This time containing the natural voices of the people I love the most embraced by sounds of a world filled with wind, birds, and music.

And sometimes, when my mom hollers my name, and I move toward the sound of her voice, I am well aware of the very special phone call waiting to hear me.

When I video call my grandmother on the phone, all I see is her ear because she wants to hear my words better. Mamá Toya loves to speak, but she loves listening even more. She loves listening to me and my sister and the way our speech is slightly mushy and our Spanish slightly tainted by an accent foreign to hers.

As I say goodbye and send my Mamá Toya besitos y abrazos, I see the gleam in my mother's eyes. She remembers how her mother has not heard our voices in person, has not listened to the melody of our song, for a very long time.

We speak strangely over there. From the last time I visited my country, I distinctly remember my cousins' words. They were haphazardly strung together and each syllable was emphasized by excitement. They speak very fast. My heartbeat rises from simply trying to follow along, and soon my tongue is smacking against my teeth as I work to imitate their exact way of speaking. It remains difficult.

Sometimes I find it hard to keep up with the euphonies of the Spanish language. The various accents and elocutions that fill my ears, overwhelm me. My mouth attempts to mimic these sounds, yet I can't help feeling like it's not enough. As if my tongue cannot move a certain way and I will never be able to match these accents and elocutions. As if I will never be able to speak as perfectly or as quickly as my cousins. As if my grandmother will never be able to hear me while she holds my hand in her palm again. Yet, my mother's laugh still harmonizes with the birds, and my dad's karaoke still echoes horrendously during Christmas. And I follow along but it's not easy. It is harder when my house is filled with Spanglish. Yet our language still sounds like a song.

THE REAL ARMY

SHANTI ARIKER

It was November 1987. I was in the women's barracks, just south of the Lebanese border in the last year of my Israeli army service. The barber, who looked the most terrified of everyone, was the only man in a room filled with female soldiers. There had been no major terror attacks since earlier in the year, and I hadn't been thinking anything like that would happen to me, but here I was in the middle of one. I had just arrived at the base a few hours ago and didn't know anyone.

~

The year before, I moved to Israel from Northern California after finishing high school in January of my senior year. This had put into place a plan started in my preteen years, during an extended family trip to Israel. My parents had decided our family would make *aliyah*, which literally means *to go up*, a way of saying we were going to live in Israel as soon as I completed high school. My family had rediscovered Judaism, becoming modern Orthodox Jews around when I was in kindergarten. Moving to Israel was a natural progression of the family's return to Judaism.

I left my family in California a few months ahead of their move and headed to Kibbutz Sde Eliyahu, a communal farm in the Bet She'an Valley. Sde Eliyahu had about 130 modern Orthodox families, lots of date trees, cows, horses, and vineyards on a nice spread of land. It was located in Northern Israel, on the Jordanian border, in an area that was lush and green when it rained, breezy but never too cold.

Most men on the kibbutz had beards but nothing too long and scraggly. They wore knitted *kippot*, or skullcaps, pinned to the side or backs of their heads. They wore work clothes and you could just see the *tzitziot*, or knotted fringes, peeking out of their shirts, to remind them of the 613 commandments in the Torah. Women wore both skirts and pants, which were allowed here. Some married women covered their heads with a scarf but let wisps of their hair show. Others weren't as modest and wore their hair down and uncovered, so you couldn't tell who was married or not just by how they wore their hair. The kibbutzniks celebrated all the Jewish holidays and kept the Jewish Shabbat every week, praying at a synagogue on the kibbutz, men in the front near the ark that held the Torah. The women sat behind a divider but could still be seen by the men if they glanced over their shoulders toward the back of the building.

I began in an ulpan, a residential program where a group of new immigrants live on the kibbutz and learn Hebrew. We studied half the day and worked the rest to earn our keep. I sometimes watched the kibbutz children and made breakfast for them, since they lived in dorms away from their parents. Otherwise, I was tasked with helping in the kitchen or sorting carrots for export on a conveyor belt, which was my favorite work assignment.

The carrots would fall down through a large sorting contraption and then be funneled to several conveyor belts where I sat on a stool near my other ulpan participants. Johnny and I sat across from each other, bopping our heads to the music coming from Reshet Gimel, the pop radio station, headsets over our ears to cover the loud sounds of the machines. We would sing English pop songs and watch a stream of orange move down in front of us, while we tried to quickly pick out the rocks, roots and torn carrots from the nicer carrot specimens that would be exported to Europe.

I was paired with a kibbutz family, and every Saturday during Shabbat I would spend meals and time off with them. They were originally from Sydney, Australia, and had moved to Israel about ten years before. There were three blond curly-haired kids—a boy around fifteen years old, and two younger sisters, both elementary school age. I sat in their house one Shabbat, weighing my future plans. My adopted family convinced me I should stay on Ma'aleh Gilboah, the kibbutz on the hill nearby that housed an army unit as part of the *Nahal* program. Many kibbutz kids headed to Nahal, known in English as the Pioneering Youth, since its mission back in the Eighties and before was to continue the kibbutz movement and the communal way of living. At that time, the army also created units made up entirely of new immigrants who would serve together in Nahal, the idea being that it would be easier to adjust to army life together with other immigrants.

After the ulpan was over, I entered Nahal, and on the first day, I was thrown into a hodgepodge of nationalities. We were sent to a special pre-boot camp for new immigrants to learn about the army before the regular boot camp, where we would be mixed with Israelis. Our *garin*, "seed" in Hebrew, was made up randomly grouped new immigrants. My tent housed the girls from my garin, all modern Orthodox like me, and made up of a few other Americans: two sisters originally from Brooklyn and their friend who they had grown up with in a settlement north of Jerusalem. There were also two British girls and another one from India.

In the larger unit that also slept in our tent, we had Italians, Swiss, Germans, other Brits, and South Americans, along with a few South Africans—Jews from all over the diaspora. I had never met people from most of those countries. We were supposed to speak Hebrew to each other, but it was easier to communicate with each other in English, spoken in a variety of sometimes hard-to-understand accents.

On our first day at our international boot camp, we learned to shoot a gun at a person-shaped target, not what I had expected, and we took turns staying up all night to guard our tent. I learned that I could fall asleep standing up in a full uniform with my Uzi submachine gun strapped on over my shoulders. I wasn't used to being on call all the time and paying attention extra carefully to be able to understand the Israelis barking orders at us in Hebrew.

In daytime, we marched around the large base over and over, chanting in Hebrew "left, left, left, right, left, no one speak, left, right, left," which rhymes in Hebrew. We passed other units doing the same thing in the opposite direction, as we moved under shaded areas and parts of the base that seemed to be a vehicle storage area, with lines and lines of olive green jeeps parked off the streets where we marched on the base. I was so tired after all that marching. One night, I fell asleep for eight hours straight, fully clothed in my uniform, jacket and heavy boots, gun strapped over my shoulder and lying on my belly.

We had two female commanders who wore mirrored aviator sunglasses like Tom Cruise in the movie *Top Gun* so we couldn't see their eyes and made us feel like we were doing everything wrong or too slow. The minutes of each day seemed to creep by, as we sat in the tent listening to our commanders explain each new task to us. They taught us Hebrew army slang, words we had never heard before, which would come in handy later. They taught us that the round symbols on the general's shoulders were oak leaves but people called them *falafels* because they looked like falafel balls. They taught us words like *doogri,* which means to tell it like it is and what a *jobnick* was, a soldier who got a kushy placement and was able to go home every day. They also led us through drills: how to take apart our guns, how to clean them, how to put our guns back together, where to lock our guns at the end of our beds. The commanders treated us like their wards, always serious and never smiling.

After our new immigrant training, our garin was sent to a regular boot camp. Now we were in a sea of girls, immigrants and hundreds of Israeli girls. Our group was religious but the rest of the girls were mainly secular. We no longer had tents but instead were placed in barracks with at least forty girls to a room full of bunk beds. There were row after row of barracks, at least fifteen or twenty buildings, one after the other among the trees that helped keep areas shaded where we stood at attention for various drills and inspections. All the barracks looked alike, and I had to rely on the numbers to remember where my bed was located. Each day, we would have to be awake and ready by five a.m. for our first inspection of the day.

The Israeli girls were not what I was expecting. My perception of the army was based on the US army, a volunteer army, made up of women who self-selected into that life. The stereotype I believed was that those female soldiers were less feminine. My perception was thrown off immediately. In Israel, because army service is mandatory, every type of girl serves in the army and in boot camp, I saw girls from all walks of life and from all over Israel. Girls who were sephardic Jews, whose families originated in Morocco or Yemin, with long dark curly hair, wild and puffy, some with heavy make-up and long fake nails. Others had lighter skin, blonde hair and blue eyes, with their hair in ponytails and no make-up. Some rich, some poor, all thrown together in one big boot camp.

The hardest thing to do in the mornings was get all the girls in the entire bunk area to agree on what to wear. We had three kinds of shirts, and we were all supposed to match our clothing. At least a quarter of the girls would get up at four a.m. to put on make-up and do their hair. I was not going to be one of those, as I would prefer to sleep-in than worry about what I looked like. Each patrol elected a leader and the leaders met in the morning. They conducted intense negotiations on how we would dress for the day and after that word would go around the barracks. A few days there were arguments over the different shirts but after a few days, the girls fell in line and stopped complaining.

Boot camp came and went like a dream. There were endless uniform inspections, weapon inspections, bed inspections, and canteen inspections. Israel is a hot and dry country and it was imperative that your canteen be full at all times. Throughout the day, we would be required to stop and drink at least half at a time.

We graduated in a short ceremony and were then told to meet up with our original units. Our unit was sent back to Kibbutz Ma'aleh Gilboa, on a ridge on the Gilboa Mountains. The men in our unit remained in an extended boot camp and training, where they learned how to be paratroopers. They had several required plane jumps, something I was glad that as a female I would avoid. At Ma'aleh Gilboa, I worked in the kitchen, sitting on top of a milk crate, peeling the hundreds of potatoes on hand every day for dinner, picked fresh from the nearby fields.

Once the men completed their boot camp and paratrooper training, our garin and two others boarded buses for a base about forty minutes South of the Bet She'an Valley. Our modern orthodox unit was placed in charge of a training settlement that was situated along the Jordanian border and the river valley, just north of the Occupied Territory line.

In our practice settlement, there were no cooks or drivers, as is standard in the real army. Instead, like in a settlement, our unit was to take on the different tasks required to run the place. When we weren't working in the kitchen or doing laundry, we were on guard duty up on the roof, which looked directly at a base over the border in Jordan.

We also supported our settlement's upkeep by earning money. Our unit ran a small preexisting zoo, a donkey, a few goats, and a sheep, nothing out of the ordinary as far as animals go; the stuff you generally see in petting zoos for kids. Since we would only be on the base for six months, we continued the programs started by other units who came before us. As they had, we sewed *sharwalim*, a kind of Bedouin pants for women that have billowy legs that puff out and a low crotch seam made from light cotton. We also took old heavy wooden barrels that we could source from a local kibbutz and sawed them into seats. We were allowed off the settlement base from time to time to sell our items at local markets. With the money we earned, we fed the animals, bought more supplies and created more items to sell.

After the settlement part of the Nahal program ended, we moved to Kibbutz Tirat Tzvi, which was one of the oldest ones in the country. It was next to Sde Eliyahu but more established and considered a rich kibbutz, with a beautiful pool, a large social hall and a meat factory which brought in a lot of extra money. There were about two hundred fifty families and they also housed city kids like us as well as kids from other programs.

At this point in my army service, I was getting antsy. I had joined the army to be Israeli like everyone else there, and because it had sounded exciting and exotic. Working on a kibbutz all day with a bunch of foreigners and cleaning up after ten-year-olds was neither exciting nor exotic. The girls in my garin had become two factions and I wasn't interested in socializing much with either one of them. So I transferred out of Nahal, not really understanding what would be in store for me.

~

It took about a week or two to get all the paperwork filled out for the real army. Israeli bureaucracy is absurd with no seeming logical justification. When my parents eventually left the country, I had to rework the family paperwork—my dad was still listed head of household. As a result, because I wasn't noted in the file, the representative from the ministry was up in arms.

"You actually don't exist right now," he told me, looking perplexed.

"But I'm right here, standing in front of you," I laughed.

"This is serious," he said. "I don't think you understand. We need to take care of this or you have no identity, you are not a new immigrant if you aren't in the files."

That's the kind of bureaucracy I'm talking about. Luckily the army did have a record of me, but it still required paperwork. Paperwork to be stamped, filed, sent to one base and then another. Once it was all taken care of, I was told to head to a large base in Northern Israel. I headed home for the first time in a while, and then was given orders to meet at the Northern command base. From there, I was told I would be moved to a base just north of Kiryat Shemoneh, the Northernmost town in Israel. At the Northern command base, I waited until one of the clerks at the hall where they divided up the newly arrived soldiers. One of them pointed to me to go meet my ride in the front lot.

I walked over and saw a stocky, dark-haired man in an officer's uniform standing next to a dusty army jeep. He smiled and motioned for me to get in, introducing himself as Udi. It was a typical day in Israel, the hot sun beat down on us from above, the skies a heavy blue and no clouds in sight. We did get a breeze as we drove down the roads, since there were only plastic rolled up flaps on the open-air jeep. Udi asked if I wanted a cigarette and I nodded. I had picked up the smoking habit since I had been in the army and smoked *Time*, the most ubiquitous Israeli cigarettes, costing only a one-shekel coin, at the time worth about seventy-five cents. Hardly filtered, you can feel the tar entering your lungs. The rush of nicotine hits your brain just after the first inhalation and lets you feel the pleasure of the hit immediately. We smoked in silence on our way up to the base except for the occasional call-out on the military radio. The ride took about an hour.

My new base was located in what is called *the finger of the Galilee* in Hebrew, because it looks just like a finger pointing upward when you look at the map of Israel. Once there, he stopped to say hi to the soldier on duty at the gate. The soldier peeked in at me and waved, then swung open the metal gate, and we headed into the base which would be my new home.

Udi told me to get out and take my kitbag to the girls' barracks, which he pointed out to me. I dragged the big olive bag, stuffed with all my army uniforms that I had not worn for months on the kibbutz, out of the back of the jeep and across the parking lot area to the barracks. I knocked on one of the two doors and when no one answered, I entered and saw that there were six bunk beds. One bed looked free, so I threw my bag up onto the thin mattress and headed back outside for my next set of orders.

As I came back out of the building, I heard people running and pointing. I saw a short-haired, blond soldier with three stripes and a pin through the middle on his sleeve, indicating that he was a non-commissioned officer. He glanced at me curiously and then walked toward the medic office. I looked up and saw a shape in the sky and the sun reflecting off it, just before it started to descend on the area.

I heard someone say, "Look at that strange thing in the sky."

Then we heard a thump nearby and gunshots. Suddenly the wireless radio came to life with orders barked out in Hebrew, some of which I couldn't understand; it was too fast for me.

I asked the first person I saw, "What's going on?"

"Sounds like a terrorist attack," said a soldier. "Stay near the barracks until we know more."

Male soldiers started to run to different jeeps and some of the armored personnel carriers in the back of the base, which I hadn't noticed until just then. The men donned their helmets and grabbed Galil guns, the pervasive Israeli machine guns that took over from the less accurate Uzi guns that most Americans knew. They slung the guns over their shoulders with the gun butts still folded inward and headed toward the gate. About half the men were already driving past the gate, when a man wearing officer insignia on his shoulders yelled for the female soldiers to gather in the girls' barracks.

The girls soon were huddled together inside, a few sitting on folding chairs in the middle of the bunk beds, others on their mattresses. The barber sat on a chair in the middle of the room, his knees up against his chest and his boots on the chair. He had his head between his knees and looked like he was going to be sick. The male barber was the only one with a gun, but it seemed clear that he would not be any help to us if the girls were in danger. We would have to take matters into our own hands, I thought.

Sarah was the first to speak, her voice shaking. "I want to go home, I don't understand why we have to stay here if we are in danger."

"Really, Sarah, calm down," said Iris. "It's not like we can just pick up and leave, the terrorists are now to the south of us. We can't just head home anyway, you know that."

We stayed quiet, staring at nothing until Udi came in, the door swinging closed behind him.

"Hi, girls. Don't worry, things will be fine," he said, winking at the group of us.

A few looked up at him, including Sarah, and gave him an incredulous look. "I don't think I believe you right now. This is scary, I want to go home," she said.

He spoke quickly with a clipped tone. "Don't worry, it will be ok, we are getting the situation under control. How about a few of you come with me and we get some coffee started for the guys outside. We may be here all night."

I volunteered to go. I didn't want to just sit huddled around with people I had just met with all the chaos going around us outside. I was restless and wanted to get out of the building to see what was happening, if there was anything to see in the dark. I walked with a red-headed talkative girl, Nirit, toward the kitchen. We picked up a large pot, enough for making rice for twenty people and filled it with water. Then we waited for the water to boil on the stove.

Nirit chatted away while we waited, telling me she was from Ra'ananah, a middle-class town near Tel Aviv, housing mainly Jews who had arrived from Europe and increasingly native Israelis. She lived on a *moshav*, another kind of communal farm and her father ran the *refet*, a cow barn. She asked when I had arrived, and I told her that it was just before the strange things appeared in the sky. She was curious why I had shown up today but didn't ask me more, and I didn't volunteer any more information. I wanted to focus on what we were doing and not think about where I was or whether I had made a mistake by leaving the kibbutz.

When the pot was filled as much as we thought we would be able to carry, we took instant coffee and scooped in several cups full, tasting it to see if it was drinkable. When the taste was strong enough and the water looked an acceptable shade of dark brown, we each had a cup each ourselves, burning our tongues. It was bitter, but the familiar taste of Israeli instant coffee calmed my nerves. Then we took some kitchen towels and between the two of us, steadied the pot and got it off the stove. It sloshed a little, but we were able to keep it from spilling. We then walked from station to station outside and let the soldiers get a cup or two. We continued to walk around with the coffee, meting it out, until it was almost gone, and we could pour the final amount into a cup and give that away to the nearest soldier.

While we doled out the coffee, Nirit and I learned what had happened. Two terrorists had flown hang gliders over the border from Southern Lebanon, and that was the strange shape we had seen far up in the sky. One of the men had landed just below our base near a second base closer to the city. The front gate guard was surprised and shot immediately by the terrorist who then got onto the base and opened fire on a dozen more soldiers, killing several before he was finally shot and killed. The second hang-gliding-terrorist that had landed further south and our base had sent in search of him.

Dawn was starting to break and I really wanted to sleep, but I hadn't set up my bed yet and everyone was still in our room. At around five a.m., Udi, the officer who had brought me to the base, came back in and announced that everything was over. Soldiers had found the last terrorist.

At seven a.m., we were allowed to call our parents and tell them we were fine but not anything else. I wasn't sure that would make my family feel better, hearing from me that I was fine but without understanding why I was calling so early in the morning. I hadn't been in Israel long enough to understand that the news would be out and when they heard about it, they would already know not to worry.

After that, despite hearing my stomach growl, I headed to my barracks. On the way, I saw a blonde soldier I had met briefly when meting out coffee. He's the cute one, I thought. We nodded at each other. I smiled and he smiled back. I opened the door to our room in the barracks, got out of the clothes I had been wearing since I arrived, quickly slapped a sheet onto my bed and climbed onto the thin mattress on the top bunk. I was soon asleep but not before wondering if I'd made a mistake by leaving the relative safety of the kibbutz for a spot on the Northern border in the real army. Or maybe I was becoming a real soldier.

ON TONI MORRISON'S *BELOVED*

ANNE RAEFF

Two years ago, tired of being in a perpetual state of anger about the state of the world and the United States especially, my wife, Lori, and I decided that we needed a different approach to life. We needed to do something we had never done before, something that would give us purpose and from which we could learn in a new, not an intellectual, way. Over the years of our relationship—we have been together for twenty-eight years—we sometimes talked about adopting a child or fostering, but we enjoyed the freedom and focus on our work and writing that childlessness provided, so the conversations never were very serious. But this time, when my wife, Lori, mentioned fostering, we kept on talking about it, imagining what it would be like. We took the first steps. We filled out the paperwork. We did the trainings, the house checks, the psychological interviews. We said we were open to any child from the age of six and onward, but we indicated on the forms that we might be a good fit for an LGBTQ+ child. We knew these young people were especially at risk.

Finally, in January of 2019 we were approved and in March our son, J, came to live with us. He was fourteen at the time and will be turning sixteen in July. In September we will become his legal guardians. Soon after he moved in, as part of our campaign to get him back into reading, we started a custom of reading out loud after dinner. We started with *Night*, his choice. (He likes intense books.)

Then, in the fall of 2019, the three of us, two middle-aged white lesbians and a young African American gay boy, began reading *Beloved* by Toni Morrison. We took it slowly, savoring the poetry, reading it as one should read all great books, as if there were no other. Yet there were nights when the intensity of the cruelty and suffering that Morrison writes about made it impossible for us to bear reading more than two or three pages at a time. At one point when J's emotions were especially raw, we took a week off. The book brought to the surface all the trauma that he had experienced as a black man in America and all the trauma that he had inherited from his ancestors.

Though we were experiencing the book together, though the book brought us together in new ways, it also emphasized our differences very clearly—J is black and we are white. Racial injustice and white supremacy make our experiences in the world vastly different, and we all understand that these injustices are what led J to be taken from his family, what led him to us, to sitting with us in our living room reading *Beloved*. But still we kept reading through the thick pain of the story, the history that is a part of us all.

I have chosen the following section precisely because, in it, the past and the present are one. It demonstrates perhaps better than any piece of prose ever written the weight of history that we must bear, that we cannot throw off even when we are looking it in the eye. This passage, which takes place toward the end of the book, illustrates the omnipresence of the past in all stories. In this case Sethe, the hero of the book, is reliving the experience of her ancestors during the Middle Passage and yet there is a scent of a time before when there were flowers and sweet smells and songs. It is a passage full of the ghosts that live within us and around us still:

> In the beginning the women are away from the men and the men are away from the women   storms rock us and mix the men into the women and the women into the men   that is when I begin to be on the back of the man   or a long time I see only his neck and his wide shoulders   above me   I am small   I love him because he has a song   when he turned around to die I see the teeth he sang through   his singing was soft   his singing is of the place where a woman takes flowers away from their leaves and puts them in a round basket   before the clouds   she is crouching near us   but I do not see her until he locks his eyes and dies on my face   we are that way   there is no breath coming from his mouth and the place where breath should be is sweet-smelling   the others do not know he is

dead   I know   his song is gone   now I love his pretty little
teeth instead

I cannot lose her again   my dead man was in the way like
the noisy clouds   when he dies on my face I can see hers she
is going to smile at me   she is going to   her sharp earrings
are gone   the men without skin are making loud noises they
push my own man through   they do not push the woman with
my face through   she goes in   they do not push her   she goes
in   the little hill is gone   she was gong to smile at me she was
gong to   a hot thing

It was not until I began writing my first book—which was based
on my family history, their flight from war and persecution, their
experiences in what history calls the Holocaust but which is, in fact,
millions of individual stories bound together by grief and cruelty—that
I understood there was no distinction between story and history, between
present and past. When I was growing up, the people who populated
the stories my parents and grandparents told me were as real to me, as
present, as my teachers and my school friends, so present that sometimes
just as Sethe in *Beloved* talks to her ghosts, I spoke to my dead. I spoke
to my father's brother who died of starvation and cold in Siberia. I spoke
to the prisoner of war at the POW camp in Arizona where my father was
an interpreter, who thought that Stalin was living in his brain. I spoke
to my grandmother's mother, who left them one day, ran off and was
never seen again, to my father's childhood friend who died silently from
asphyxiation due to a gas leak while taking a bath in Lisbon. I imagined
her sinking into the warm water. I felt her body finally relax after months
of fear, of waiting for the Nazis to find them, of the long journey through
France and Spain.

Though this unity of present and past, story and history has always
been true, perhaps we as a nation are beginning to see this truth. Since the
first Europeans set foot in the Americas, the culture of the United States,
of all the Americas, has been based on ignoring history, on attempting to
erase indigenous culture and covering up the inhumanity of slavery. The
wealthy and privileged have focused on amassing more and more wealth
while the poor and unprivileged focused on dreaming of riches. Now we
are taking a moment to acknowledge the past and the role it plays in the

present. Perhaps now we will be able to tell stories in which the past and the present cannot be separated from each other, in which history and story are one and the same.

In my latest book, *Only the River*, past and present flow together down the San Juan River, into the town of El Castillo along the banks of the river, through the lives of two families, one Jewish refugees and one Nicaraguan. Here is the first description of that town where past and present are one. In it Pepa, who when she was an adolescent lived for a few years in El Castillo with her parents and brother after escaping Vienna and the Holocaust, lulls her adult-daughter, Liliana, to sleep by invoking the river as she had done when Liliana and her brother were children:

"Listen to the motor and the lapping of the water against the lancha. There on the right bank are some herons sunning themselves. Now you are coming around the bend. Soon you will see the Spanish fortress on top of the hill. It's so big the houses of the village look like toys in comparison. Look at the houses, all those colors. Ours is pink, but can't see it from the river. Can you hear the falls? The lancha is approaching the dock now. There is Don Solano's shop and there is the church. Don't take your hand out of the river, not until you're there, not until the lancha has pulled into the dock and the driver cuts the motor. Sleep," she said. "You are safe now," Pepa whispered as she did when they were children. "Sleep."

SIMPSON WRITING WORKSHOP

GIRLS INC.—ALAMEDA COUNTY

UTTARA CHINTAMANI CHAUDHURI,

SIMPSON FELLOW

1. The Unstoppable Woman

By Amira Jourdan

A woman takes each step
With a sense of pride.
She walks with some pep,
Hands swaying at her sides.

Her stride so nonchalant,
She is a fierce lioness.
Her confidence she flaunts
Without a hint of shyness.

2. Untitled

By Dallas Panopio

As I waited for my friends at the end of the hallway,
She pulled me aside
And said she had something for me.

Pulling out a piece of paper with a plastic ring taped to it,
Reading the chorus to my favorite song,
A smile took over my face.

Such a grandiose gesture
Her heart was gold
Just like the song.

I knew it was cheap, but I still wore it.

3. *Untitled*

By Esmeralda Pedroza

I love myself and I am more than enough,
I will always be more than enough.
I believe in myself and what I can accomplish.
I accept myself with all my flaws and imperfections,
The same that have shaped and rounded me to be who I am today.
I am proud to be the strong, independent, and outspoken young
woman I am.

People may ask, what is the true meaning of life?
What is the purpose of the ocean, sun, and all of God's creations?
Seeking help in a world full of loss,
In desperation, I gaze at God's creations.
Blank stares but no answers to all my questions,
Silent as a forgotten melody.
I lie there helpless.

The wind blows against my face,
Closing my eyes, I lose all my fears.
The humid sand is soft beneath my feet,
I watch time fly as the waves crash into the rocks.
As the birds soar in the clear blue sky,
As the sun begins to set, the skies cry,
In red, yellow, and orange shades of tears.
The sun shines through the clouds like a seashell in the sand,
The sun-kissed yellow glow makes me feel safe, creating warmth.

I wish you had never closed your eyes,
The longest exhale I've ever heard.
Not knowing it would be your last breath,
I heard the last sigh of relief.
With your departure, you took a part of me,
I was left in the world; lonely, lost, and fearful.
I still remember you and your ways,
Those irreplaceable Friday nights, eating ice cream,

Talking about life and how weird we both were.
I take you with me everywhere I go,
You will always be a part of me, *mejor amigo*.

As the night draws to an end,
I look up to the luminous stars in awe,
Answers sent from God in his creations,
To live life as if there is no tomorrow,
To love, accept, and enjoy life and God's creations to fullness.

4. *They Believed Otherwise*

By Izba Haq

just embrace yourself they said—
but the media says otherwise
perfect bodies, perfect hair
glowy skin
little cares

just embrace yourself they said—
but society demands otherwise
eat more, eat less
cover up
act like the rest

just embrace yourself they said—
but they believed otherwise
which lead to their
untimely demise

5. *Untitled*

By Jasmin Jacobo

I stand outside and see the sky
Seeing the birds flying high
I hear the birds chirp like never before
As I walk back through my front door

I sit, then lie down on my bed
And think about everything in my head
Letting all the thoughts fly around
Feeling myself to be earthbound

6. *Untitled*

By JoAnne Ohwobete

You spend your nights playing scenario
after scenario, one by one,
hoping
no
praying
that the angel on your shoulder
speaks louder than the devil
just this once.
The thoughts are unwanted waves
crashing against a shore
at high tide.
You spend your nights playing scenario
after scenario, one by one,
until you don't.

7. Times We Are Living In

By Morgan Vincent

Why are these days going so slow,
As if we are in some kind of show.
Inside a movie to which we were sent,
Where COVID-19 is the main event.

This all started at the end of 2019,
When everyone was as happy as can be.
Until the media showed a disease so unseen,
An unseen disease ended our dream.

Will everything go back to normal,
When this pandemic is over?
Or will everything stay the same,
As if COVID-19 never came.

Will people continue to keep six feet apart?
Or will they have a change of heart?
I just pray that those who are ill recover,
So they have the chance to see another summer.

Six weeks of quarantine passed by so fast,
Yet COVID-19 is still not the past.

8. How I've Felt During COVID-19

By Ngalifourou Matingou

I can't sleep, but why do I weep
Is it the late night calls, or the barricades
But why do I weep, why, you say?
It is the loneliness, or is it stress,
I have blurred my identity.
Who am I, I've lost myself.
But I still can't sleep.

9. Untitled

By Asha Dunn

The boat ride to our new home was nothing short of abysmal. For six days and six nights we endured the sad rocking of a cold wet ship, with just enough of our belongings to carry on our backs. It was only my mother, sister, and I facing the wrath of our reality, hanging on to only our hope of a new life.

I don't remember much of my homeland. Yet I can recall soft, warm beaches with water passing for miles, the sweet sound of my mother's lullaby as I ate fried plantains and warm milk, and a happy house where we sang and danced as a family. Those good memories are easy to reminisce in, but the bad ones are still hard to forget.

I remember the violence. I was only three when I saw my first dead body. There are many ways that I've seen it be done: hacked, mutilated, shot, or stabbed, all in a continuous war between neighboring gangs and families. All while innocent lives were constantly being caught up in all the horror. When I walked outside after the noise, I saw him bleeding out into the sand. My mother had no idea where I was. I called out to him. "Papa" I said. No response. Again, "Papa." Nothing.

My bare feet sunk into the wet blood-drenched sand. I saw a single tear run down his face as I laid my head on his chest with his hand in mine for his last moments of serenity. I felt the life leave his hand as I held it and when my mother found me, she had to rip me from his body because I didn't want him to be alone. From that day forward the violence never let up and by the time I was five years old, I would find myself in the lower wet deck of a sad ship, huddled with my mother and sister on our way to America. I thought it would be everything I wished for, and at the time it was. When we arrived in Florida, I once again got to feel the comfort of a welcoming beach and I believed I could make this my new home.

As the years passed, we gathered enough money to move from our small house off the coast in Miami to Bluewater California, and oh was it beautiful! Trees that reached the sky, water like a bath, and an everlasting hug from the sun. Again, I thought it was perfect, but even my young mind could understand the upgrade from my previous standard of living. And from that day forward I've called this place home. But even though on the outside my life now seems like it should be happy and fair; over the years I began to notice something that I long to escape. I'm sixteen and I know now that the war we fled, that started my family's internal suffering, is here. And it always has been—just in a different form that I was unable to recognize until now.

I came to a new world filled with racism and discrimination that I had never seen before. Before coming to America, I was never made fun of for my dark complexion and curly hair. I didn't understand how they could so easily despise the Jamaican-American child I had become, until I realized how deep the hatred runs in our history. The pain and discomfort we bring each other as humans is woven into our past but there's no reason that it has to be passed on into our future.

From all the blood-shed and battles I've seen; I've learned that the cycle must stop. But my problem is that I have no idea how. I know there are millions of other people in the world who understand my struggle and the challenges I've had to overcome and even more who can see the ignorance in mankind. I realize that the only way to succeed and fight through the harshness we call reality is to find a connection through the hurt rooted in the same cause. But how do I reach them?

For now, I can try to get my voice heard but I have to remember it's not just my voice. No—it's the voice of reason, of true humanity, of kindness and experience. How is it that I am only sixteen and I can see the corruption that most adults can't? Where does that put me in society? It puts me at the bottom of a very long totem pole, but I know if I focus and I try and I never give in to the endless cycle of negativity, I can get it done. We can, together. My name is Sabine King and mine is just one story among many. I know that I'll never give up and neither should you.

NOTES ON THIS TIME FROM MY ETERNAL CITY

T. GERONIMO JOHNSON

The search for a metaphor to structure this piece was in vain. Our social challenges feel too wide-ranging to submit to a unified figurative vision.

I often begin with a metaphor to define the contours of the inciting abstraction. I have a feeling, an experiential understanding that bridges emotion and intellect, and figurative language carries that over to another human. Readers translate the text into their private emotional language. *Mine* becomes *ours*.

Likewise, when I read, another human's experiences, thoughts, and feelings are witnessed, pondered, incorporated. *Yours* becomes *mine*.

Even if I cannot consciously recall the text, I will never forget. That contact with another human mind, across space and time, will always remain a part of me—whether it's Baldwin, Shakespeare, or the purported author of a sacred text.

Influence persists. That's one of the most profound wisdoms of the human vessel; nothing is forgotten but fortunately everything is not recalled. To imagine otherwise is to imagine being swamped by the raw experience of others—good and bad—to the point of dysfunction. Thank Freud for the ego, which one undergrad professor described as the "necrotic layer that protects the self from the deluge of life." In the expanded metaphor the ego is a scaly exoskeleton without which the mental body would be permeated by the outer environment—*flooded*. She went on to explain it as a sieve filtering out potentially damaging sediment. Both analogies echo our vernacular notions of how the mind works.

It safeguards us from inconvenient knowledge, even when that knowledge is a manifest, firsthand, immediate experience that triggers every sense organ. The mind protects us from insights that destabilize our world view and our role on that stage.

Enter here art. Art slips through the filters. Art is the most vital and direct form of human communication. Literature is the most intimate and immersive art because language is the sense organ we share.

Someone who is reading will accept that immediately. Others will ruminate, ponder, contemplate. An alarming number will contest, not out of any solid objection, out of habit. I suggest not giving it a second thought and observing *how the mind.* I have noticed in many conversations lately a phenomenon those of a certain generation would recognize as *Duck Season, Rabbit Season.*

In a *Looney Tunes* episode, Elmer Fudd is hunting and encounters Bugs Bunny and Daffy Duck. A debate ensues between the two potential targets. Is it duck season or is it rabbit season? Both targets stand their ground until Bugs Bunny modifies his rhetorical strategy. He concedes that it's rabbit season, signifying that he is Elmer Fudd's legitimate and legal target. Daffy Duck objects and insists that it's duck season. It you don't know this cartoon, watch it. There are three versions. In at least one version, Bugs and Daffy pivot the barrel of Elmer's shotgun as they argue. When Bugs the *bunny* holds the shotgun to his chest and declares it to be rabbit season, Daffy the *duck* snatches the barrel away so that it's pointed to his face, yells, "Duck season, fire!"

Elmer fires. Daffy is blasted, his face blown black by scattershot.

I promise that if you start to listen closely, you will observe that this discourse pattern emerges with alarming frequency. Not everyone yells *Fire!*, but you will be amazed at the number of folks who only think that it's Rabbit Season until *"certain people"* about whom they feel a *"certain way,"* agree. Then it's Duck Season.

Replace *certain* as you see fit. The more pressing question: *What is the gun?*

As I writer I've always been interested in Kierkegaard's notion that those influences of which we are unaware have the greatest command. What does Daffy Duck want? The terms of most debates reflect only superficial considerations. In the sandbox of political semantics, in the era of dog whistle politics, language itself is increasingly less important than what it points to, be it emotional, psychological, or semantic. The chasm has grown between denotation and connotation, usurped by rabid zeal. Daffy Duck doesn't want it to be Rabbit Season as much as Daffy Duck wants to be right. Daffy Duck's oppositional animosity toward Bugs Bunny explodes the bounds of logic, leaving him in a baffled state where his survival drive is trumped by his lust for Bugs' sole possession in that moment when the rabbit possesses nothing other than a loaded gun pointed at this chest.

There are ways in which we all do this, but again, there's a more pressing question: *What is the gun over which you are fighting?*

I know. You do, too. I am not going to tell you, because the ego does not work in mysterious ways. If I share the answer, you will not let the answer in. But if you answer for yourself, you might let the answer out.

I'll put it like this: *By who is it that we clamor to be shoot, elbowing each other out of the way as if a bullet wound was a frameable autograph?*

We must be ever vigilant about the truth of this world. Racism is not an American disease. America springs from a colonial petri dish in which anti-blackness was vital to social, economic, and spiritual health, but racism is not an American disease. Colonialism defines the entire post-Enlightenment project. History is not without its rewards; rewards are not without sacrifices.

But before that, way before that, came linear thinking, Christian eschatology, and the promise of a City on Hill in which the blessed would luxuriate while the wicked burn for eternity. That's a long time. You should call a friend if you believe vast swatches of humanity deserve to burn in hell forever. A few, maybe, *but on the biblical scale condoned by the sacred text? Eternal suffering without any opportunity to be redeemed?* That sounds alarmingly like the internet, though none of us techies would call ourselves fundamentalists.

Before the Bible was the Epic of Gilgamesh, the eternally relevant treatise on friendship and mortality. We think, most of us, we are modern and rational and righteous. But we are all complicit in the hubris of modernity. Some us are also Gilgamesh mourning the loss of his friend Enkidu. But in this case, Enkidu is the inner self that knows better, the self that remains undistracted by capitalism, remains hopeful, remains invested in vital and authentic connection—digital or otherwise.

The Time's Literary Supplement recently published an article entitled, *The Internet is a Capricious and Angry God.* You can anticipate the argument, and would likely deem it sound. Today people can be summarily sentenced to social death, and left with no way to repay the alleged debt to society because infractions are forever, while apologies are fragile things of no abiding interest. But the Internet is not an angry and capricious god anymore more than the flood in Genesis is an angry and capricious deluge. We are the angry and capricious gods. Each of us. And this is the world we have made. Hence the pitfalls to date of outsourcing sentencing and hiring to AI.

Our next conversation must explore disregard for human rights as the disease ravaging every inefficient or poisonous system we encounter or inhabit, from the prison system to public schools to the environment. And we are each complicit because eventually the oppressed become complicit in their own oppression. How else are we to survive?

During a recent panel on race and literature, a white male inquired about a litmus test for determining his complicity in white supremacy (white heteropatriarchy). I did not tell him the truth, that by virtue of my participation in the system, even sitting on that panel, though I may wish it were otherwise, I was complicit. As a university professor, I am complicit. As a writer working in English, I am complicit. As an American, I am complicit. If I proselytize for white Jesus, I am doubly complicit. Assimilation, that survival instinct, even when provisionally or periodically embraced, is complicity.

My novels explore how that conscription into complicity operates at a frequency beyond conscious perception, for people of all races. There is no way that white America can be waking up for the first time. So I ask you, and me, and everyone else this: *What else are you sleeping through?*

And we are all asleep to someone's pain. Most adults are teenagers on life support.

We have abandoned hopes, dreams, loves, wishes. Abandoned, but not forgotten.

It's easier to forget, but more rewarding to engage those hopes, dreams, loves, wishes, and the uncertainty they raise. This is what I feel every time I write, extreme discomfort, because I have always written about race, gender, and other politicized identities as they are experienced, not through a lens of aspiration. This has not proven a remunerative aesthetic choice. Publishers have not wanted to pay for books that failed to reflect their myopic illusion of the contemporary American meritocracy. As I was once told, it would be good for my career if my next book wasn't about race.

Enter here the Simpson/JCO Prize. Art can lead the way, but the way forward requires a step back, discomfiting reflection, a bitter acknowledgement about who we are. Racism, sexism, homophobia, educational pedigree-ism, fool us into thinking capitalism is an equitable system. Under those blinders are others.

As I work to remove my many blinders, those I wear as a parent, a writer, a member of the human community, I endeavor to ask questions without easy answers, of myself and in my work. This does not always make for popular fiction. The Simpson/JCO Prize is a welcome laurel, an imprimatur. The financial prize supports intellectual inquiry, creative freedom, interrogation of spirit, lots of diapers. Most importantly, it buys time, without which my new novel could not have been written. Will this novel, about a couple who find themselves "unwitting" cogs in a brutal machine, land on your desk, shelf, or e-reader? Will mine become yours? I certainly hope so. If it does, that's in no small part thanks to this award.

The challenge soon facing us won't be excising obvious expressions of white supremacy, statues, laws, hiring practices; it will be excising white supremacy from passive and active perpetrators on both sides of the aisle. How will you know what that looks like? Will you let Bugs be shot? Will you swing the muzzle to your own face? Will you call off the hunt?

Extinguishing anti-blackness, racism, sexism, and other prejudicial biases will not make capitalism equitable. Defunding police departments will not eradicate the pathology of American violence. Dismantling prisons will not make us more merciful. These things must happen as soon as possible. Yet, work will remain, for you, and for me.

"LIFE ITSELF IS A QUOTATION" (JORGE LUIS BORGES)

MICHAEL ROSS

I believe my earliest introduction to reading was seeing how both my parents read regularly during leisure time. I do not recall much of what they read, but I think my mother preferred lighter fare, such as popular mysteries, while my father read more serious works, including Shakespeare's plays.

Isn't it funny how paradise always lies in the past or the future, never exactly in the present? JOHN UPDIKE, S

I made my way through high school English classes with moderate success. I majored in English in college based upon a friend's advice that it had the fewest required courses. In preparation for third- and fourth-year comprehensive exams, I took a variety of courses, including The Novel, Shakespeare, Victorian Literature, and Modern Poetry, all of which I enjoyed. I was, however, spared from having to prove my knowledge of these works because "comps" were abolished in both my third and fourth years.

"The only thing I know for sure is you can never be too misinformed." RICHARD POWERS, *Generosity, an Enhancement*

My next four years were spent in the Navy, making one tour in the Pacific and two in the Mediterranean. I reckon that about half my time was at sea, affording me a great deal of time to read at least some of the books I neglected in college. It was during this time that I began collecting quotations simply for my own enjoyment and edification.

You can't keep on talking forever about what a hell of a good time you had when you were kids. ROBERT PENN WARREN, *All the King's Men*

I continued avidly reading literary fiction during law school, despite very heavy reading assignments, and my legal career, the reading for which dwarfed the loads in law school. After my legal employment, I taught practical seminars in the US and in China, Croatia, and Spain. During all these endeavors, I found that my extracurricular reading of literary fiction enhanced my performance and experiences.

But my experience is that as soon as people are old enough to know better, they don't know anything at all. OSCAR WILDE, *Lady Windemere's Fan*

I think I gravitated to literary fiction because that was what I was introduced to in school and have found very rewarding over the years. I occasionally read non-fiction, such as works by Stephen Jay Gould, Lewis Thomas, and John McPhee. I sometimes feel I am missing a great deal by not reading more history, biography, and science.

He liked his enemies best because he never had to doubt their sincerity; ... ETHAN CANIN, *America America*

My early selections were predominantly white, US authors, such as, John Barth, John Gardner, Kurt Vonnegut, Philip Roth, Bernard Malamud, Saul Bellow, Gore Vidal, John Updike, Herman Wouk, Leon Uris, Wallace Stegner, Robert Penn Warren, and Walker Percy. I also read many more contemporary authors, for example, Paul Auster, Ivan Doig, Thomas Pynchon, John Gardner, William Kennedy, Richard Powers, Richard Russo, John Irving, Richard Brautigan, and T.C. Boyle. I also read many novels by British writers, including John Fowles, Anthony Burgess, Graham Greene, George Orwell, Joseph Conrad, W. Somerset Maugham, Aldous Huxley, Piers Paul Read, Richard Adams, and Kingsley Amis. I did not consciously choose to discriminate in my reading. I think I was reading then well-known and highly regarded authors, some of whom were recommended to me by reliable sources. I was relatively comfortable to keep going back to authors I liked rather than risking that the time reading new authors would be disappointing.

Not even a contortionist...could see all sides of himself at once.
IVAN DOIG, *Prairie Nocturne*

In recent years, especially since the publication of my first volume of quotes, I have endeavored to broaden my horizons, reading more female authors, such as Anne Tyler, Lorrie Moore, Madeleine L'Engle, Iris Murdoch, Doris Lessing, Elizabeth Goudge, Katherine Ann Porter, Isak Dinesen, and Willa Cather. I have also read excellent works by highly regarded foreign authors, including Carlos Fuentes, Jose Saramago, Gunter Grass, Heinrich Boll, Paul Bowles, Vladimir Nabokov, Gabriel Garcia Marquez, Milan Kundera, Nikos Kazantzakis, V.S. Naipaul, and Robertson Davies. I confess that some of this effort was driven by the passing of many of my favorite authors, such as Ivan Doig, Herman Wouk, John Gardner, Leon Uris, Peter Matthiessen, Jim Harrison, John Updike, John Fowles, Robertson Davies, and William Trevor. As I grew older, I sensed that there were so many more talented authors that I needed to experience first-hand, and I did little research on authors and books that were prize-winners and otherwise on recommended "bucket lists."

One reaches the age when being realistic isn't practical anymore. RICHARD POWERS, *Operation Gathering Soul*

Over the years, my reading practices have changed, mostly, I believe, for the better. For a long time, I felt compelled to read every book I started, even if I was not enjoying it. I have abandoned that practice and am now comfortable putting down a book that has not become interesting after a fair trial.

We wouldn't care so much what people thought of us if we knew how seldom they did. JOHN LANCHESTER, *Mr. Phillips*

Another habit I have broken is trying to read all or most of the works by an author whose first book I read and liked. This worked well for some writers, for example, Leon Uris, Robertson Davies, Richard Russo, Paul Auster, T.C. Boyle, John Hersey, Wallace Stegner, John Gardner, Walker Percy, Graham Greene, and Leon Uris, but not so well, in my opinion, for Philip Roth, John Barth, Joseph Heller, Ken Kesey, Thomas Pynchon, and Don DeLillo.

"There are few reasons for telling the truth, but for lying the number is infinite." CARLOS RUIZ ZAFON, *The Shadow of the Wind*

A relatively new practice is to read novels that are set in destinations where we will be or are traveling. Some examples include: Balzac in Paris, Bowles in Morocco, Carlos Ruiz Zafon in Barcelona, Patrick White in Australia, Halldor Laxness in Iceland, Melville in French Polynesia, Eleanor Catten, and Rose Tremain in New Zealand. I find that this enhances my enjoyment of our travels.

He never married, you know. He always said that by the time he knew the woman well enough to marry her, he knew better. JOHN STEINBECK, *The Short Reign of Pippin IV*

I usually read two or three books at a time no matter how engaging one of the books is. I like being able to put one down and pick up another, maybe just for variety, a change from classic to modern or contemporary literature or a change of place or pace.

"Very few people will turn down a direct invitation to talk about themselves." DAVID LODGE, *Home Truths*

I try not to select authors and books based upon some sense of the likelihood of finding sharable quotes. In some excellent works I find numerous quotes and in others, which I enjoy just as much, I do not find any or only a few. Some examples of the former are: Gore Vidal, Jose Saramago, John Updike, Richard Powers, and Carlos Fuentes. Examples of the latter include: Mario Vargas Llosa and Kazuo Ishiguro.

He has a good voice, but like most people with good voices or ideas that they consider good, he finds it hard to stop. JOHN HERSEY, *The Conspiracy*

It is difficult to describe concisely my criteria for selecting passages to keep and share. Generally, they are observations by the narrator, or something said or thought by a character, that jump out at me. They are pithy, thought-provoking, ironic, concise, humorous, or all of the above. My collecting is not a search, rather, as I read, I stumble across ideas that have not occurred to me, insights into simple or complex topics, challenges to my perceptions or notions that reinforce my thinking.

Marriage, she felt, was a fine arrangement generally, except that one never got it generally. One got it specifically, very specifically. LORRIE MOORE, "Real Estate," in *Birds of America*

I began jotting down quotes as I read, but that was cumbersome and interruptive. Later I dog-eared pages where I found something good. There were two problems with this: it was sometimes later difficult to find my gem, and I learned that this was not a good thing to do to hardbacks, especially first editions and other valuable copies. Now I dog-ear the pages of paperbacks and mark the quote in pencil and use Post-Its for hardbacks.

Old age takes all the fun out of trouble. EDWARD ABBEY, *Good News*

A result of the almost fifty years of collecting quotes is a large number, approximately 1600 quotes on at least forty topics, such as men, women, love, sex marriage, time, age, past present, future, memory, reality, thinking, reasoning, contemplation, personal relations, and personal communications, all of which have been included in published volumes: *Ross's Novel Discoveries, Ross's Timely Discoveries, Ross's Thoughtful Discoveries, Ross's Personal Discoveries,* and *Ross's Communicative Discoveries.*

You may think you are living in modern times, here and now, but that is the necessary illusion of every age. E. L. DOCTROW, *The Waterworks*

Turning quotes into what I hope are interesting books for avid readers and quote-lovers involves several steps. I select related topics for which I have a critical mass of quotes, usually more than 100. I pull the quotes from a master collection, organize the topics and quotes in an order that I find rational (though readers may advocate better ones). I write the introduction to the book, and as I write the introduction to each section and the comments on each quote, I reorganize the quotes. I try to offer personal commentary on each one, sometimes providing some context for the quotes.

Trying to think was like picking through a rubbish dump looking for nothing in particular. KINGSLEY AMIS, *Stanley and the Women*

I am very fond of inspiring, thought-provoking, ironic, pithy, and humorous quotes. Quotes play an important role in our formal and informal education. They can be an effective and efficient way to communicate ideas. They are often not only informative, but also entertaining. I include quotes I have collected not only to share their wisdom or lack thereof, but also to introduce readers to authors and books they may not know or know well. Collecting and reading the quotes has raised questions and reflections on my life. Publishing the volumes of quotes has given me a mission. It is very gratifying for me to learn that readers appreciate my effort.

But it often happens that talking something over with someone has the effect of clarifying one's thoughts, even if that someone merely gapes at one like a goldfish. P. G. WODEHOUSE, *A Pelican at Blandings*

So, in what sense is "life itself a quotation"? I cannot speak for Jorge Luis Borges, but I suggest that from a very early age, our lives consist of repeating what we hear and learn from others. Although we may have original ideas, they are the result of our assimilation of what we have absorbed from others during our formal and informal education, from sources such as family, friends, colleagues, adversaries, reading, the arts, and the media.

WRITING AS EXTERTIMINATING, TRAPPING, AND RELEASING

IAN S. MALONEY

I worked as an exterminator most of my life. It's certainly a part of my life I've tried to erase in the retelling, and yet the images always come creeping back. The beehive that fell on my head. The mice living in desk drawers in high-priced, skyscraper offices. The apartment infestation where the tenant slept on crushed cockroaches. The supermarket shut down and overrun with roaming rats in the ceilings. The termite drilling in 100 plus degree heat with kids dropping water balloons on me. The strange spaces I've been on the hunt: an airplane on the tarmac at JFK, the barns at Belmont, the ritzy exclusive literary and college clubs of Manhattan, the nursing homes across New York City, and the abandoned warehouses on the wharves of Brooklyn. They all had pests. Nowadays it's fashionable to call what I did pest control, as if you managed and negotiated with the roaches, rats, ants, mice, squirrels, and bees over occupancy. *Excuse me, this burrow is simply way too close to our tomatoes and cucumbers, Mr. Rat. How about a relocation? I have the perfect agent for you to speak with and some great coastal properties to consider.* And no, don't get me wrong, I'm all for integrated pest management, that industry code word for better sanitation practices and less poison. Common cleaning sense beats a douse of chemicals any day. And yet, I still think back to the 1980s when we killed. We exterminated. There's something about the word which sticks with me. A verb which means *to destroy completely*. It's a word I come back to often. Maybe it's a bar we can't guarantee with pest removal, maybe it's too loaded from human history. Or, maybe it's too apocalyptic, maybe it's not something we should ever do.

Most of the work I did as a kid was an abstraction. I walked around behind the old man and sprayed the corners and crevices of homes, restaurants, and bars. Nothing died as far as I knew, and I picked up a few dollars for comics and baseball cards. That changed one day in a posh, dimly lit club before my tenth birthday. Dad picked up a Ketchall trap with two mice in it. And we weren't leaving it there for them to starve to death and begin to rot in the trap. I sweated, kept asking endless questions, paced the room, looked to the ceiling, and prayed to God for a reprieve. For a child my age, suddenly what I did became real. Nothing ever died in front of me. This day would change that, but not how I expected. I expected Dad to crush the escaping mice with the lid. Maybe shake them to death. All possibilities were on the table, until, with a quick turn of the latch, Dad slid the lid back and let them escape. The mice ran between my legs, and I jumped as I high as I could. We laughed for a moment and I joked about going after them to save face, but I didn't laugh for long.

Dad said, "Oh, there were three in there." *Were. Past tense. Right there.* That phrase still freezes me. Somehow, everything told me not to look at the trap but I did, like when you know something terrible is about to enter your line of vision and you know you shouldn't look, but you do it anyway. This was my moment. I saw a little mouse, eaten alive by its fellow mice. There was a tail, some paws, a head. Not much more. "I guess that's how it works," Dad said, as he strolled to the trash to get rid of the carcass.

I think that's the moment I became a writer. I wondered how many people felt like I did that moment. How many had seen or felt something like this? Terrified. Shocked. Horrified. Death right before your nose. Nothing to erase the memory of the trapped, now dead cannibalized mouse. And yet, I oddly knew something important happened. My dad didn't want it, but he had a lesson to give. Yeah, this happens. The world isn't always pleasant—in fact, it can be downright nasty at its borders, edges, and dark spaces; it's filled with traps and sometimes inevitable, painful death. He wanted me to see these things, so I'd never wind up doing them the rest of my life. I learned the lesson over time and never forgot it. I kept exterminating, though.

I guess that moment made me aware of what we did. And for some time, I pushed it all back. I tried to get rid of all of it, exterminate the past as best I could. I didn't talk about it, or think much about it. But it was there, like a rat peering out from the burrow, waiting to go back and hit the food source they hit last night. It's true the pathways are engrained in their muscle memories. They run the same routes to food, over and over again, until you stop them. I kept coming back to exterminating, again and again, in my personal writing. It was in my memory, and I needed to translate what it meant to me. I felt like the rat going back to the source again and again.

I buried my exterminating stories until college. During freshmen year, I was in my writing class, dreaming of being Shakespeare, Hemingway, O'Connor, Austen, Dickinson, Melville, Fitzgerald, anyone and anything but an exterminator's son from south Brooklyn. Our assignment was a process piece. Show me what you know how to do. I knew nothing, as I joked in class. I couldn't fix a car, couldn't draw a stick figure, couldn't make a delicious meal. Just nothing came to mind. I wrote an ironic peanut butter and jelly sandwich piece, and my professor tossed it back to me, with a terse "Try again, with something that's uniquely you. Cut the nonsense."

I turned to Dad at home in Brooklyn, still working routes seven days a week so I could go to an expensive college up north.

"Why not something we did?"

All the guilt and anxiety came back. *That? That stuff was brutal, it's…*I was about to say disgusting, when I had a small revelation that it was what I was, what I did, what I needed to consider. I was something to write about, and it was in the memory of my bones.

"That's a good idea. Could work. But what? I mean…"

I can still feel that tension, sitting in Providence, RI on the phone, grabbing a pen and paper to take down some notes. *I'm really going to do this? Put this down for the class to see? I'm an exterminator's son?*

I decided to do it.

"What part? We need something with solid steps."

We brainstormed the job: rat baitings, bee treatments, termite jobs, roach infestations. We agreed on trap and release. How to Get Rid of Squirrels from Your Attic. Not too gross. A gory death typically wasn't the typical outcome. True, sometimes crazed customers wanted you to dump the squirrel in a garbage pail of water and watch it drown. *Sadists.* But, typically, you figured out where they were getting in, set up the baited trap with peanut butter and nuts, got the squirrels out and closed up the hole. You drove the trapped, scared squirrel five miles away because they had an uncanny ability to find their way back. We called it the squirrel relocation program, and Dad had moved a lot of these critters to parks and wildlife preserves.

"Do I include comedy?"

"Of course you do, boy."

So, one time, we were out all day. We picked up a squirrel on the way home. I could hear him banging around in the cage in the truck. I looked back and could see him panting. A small bloody trench was on his nose from attacking the cage. It was hot, and I was beat and thinking about what baseball games were on later, maybe I'd take a quick dip in the pool before a shower, maybe I'd meet up with some friends.

I put my work gloves on mechanically as we pulled up to Marine Park in Brooklyn. Now, if I was paying attention, common sense says aim the cage into the park, not away from it. But, I wasn't paying attention today. Dad sat in the truck, filling out paperwork. I lifted the cage out of the back, opened the latch, and the squirrel sprinted right toward the row of houses across the street. Unluckily, a lady was unloading groceries. Her door was propped open with bags, and our squirrel went right in the front.

Dad watched in horror and amazement. I stood there like a statue.

"Get in the car, NOW."

We drove to home.

"Should I go back and leave a card?"

"Dope. We need to keep you grounded not daydreaming!"

That was probably as true now as it was then.

I finished the paper and the professor loved it, including my small comic sidenotes of what not to do. Professor told me he was saving a copy for future reference. It was an important moment for me, even though I didn't fully know it back then.

I knew someday I'd be a writer. I'd share things that were best kept in the dark, most of the time. I'd find ways to understand what we exterminated and why. I also knew that sometimes those things you trapped and released often gave a look back to you, as if they knew they had been saved, had been given a new lease on life, somewhere else. So many squirrels, raccoons, and opossums, just had that pause and look moment, as they left the cage for a new abode. That look back of, another day, and trees, and grass, and water, and air. I felt that way sometimes, too. For me, I still look back on that freshman year assignment, and it was my dad, now gone ten years from us, who gave me the first chance to reflect on exterminating and trapping and how he eventually released me from my fears of self-exposure and made me a proud, working-class writer, who isn't afraid to look back on what got exterminated and what got trapped and released to find new times to consider, spaces to understand, and fresh air to breathe.

GRADUATION IN THE TIME OF COVID-19

DAVID WOOD

Kurt Vonnegut is considered by many the greatest American humorist since Mark Twain. And like Twain, he combines his humor with a scathingly simple wit and unerring moral compass. That is why I teach *Slaughterhouse Five* each year: to reveal to students that some things are simply right, and others are simply wrong. In that novel he also speaks to tremendous loss, so much loss that the main character looks at repeated death and repeats "So it goes." And as I sat at home this spring, unable to return to my classroom or my students, I read, among other things, a collection of Vonnegut graduation speeches. In many of them he speaks directly of his admiration and respect for teachers. As he says, "Only well-informed, warm-hearted people can teach others things they will remember and love." Among all the things these students lost this spring, I trust those things, things they and I will remember and love, cannot be lost.

Much has been written about the rituals and events high school seniors are missing out on this year because of the social distancing requirements placed on them to protect all of us from Covid-19. Spring sports were cancelled, many students losing out on their last opportunity to play sports with each other and for their school. Junior proms and senior balls were also cancelled; many students consider these events the social highlights of their lives that they have looked forward to for years. And their high school graduation, one of the last important rites of passage remaining in American life. Think about it. No longer does every kid in American get a driver's license at sixteen, and with it that badge of freedom and adulthood it carries. Though we have attempted to make kindergarten, fifth grade, and eighth grade graduations important milestones that mark important changes in the students' lives, they are not. Students still live at home, return to a school in their neighborhoods the next year with, for the most part, the same students and friends. Life remains basically the same. High school graduation is different. After this year many students will never go to school with the same group of students again. Many will leave home, often times moving to another community or state to go to college. They become adults, and most will disappear from each other's lives. This year the ritual that marks these changes for them will be virtual. They will not walk across that stage in front of their families and teachers, jump and throw their mortarboards with their friends or punch beach balls, they will not hug their loved ones in public.

On June 3 for the first time in over two months I drove to Northgate High School, where I have been teaching for thirty-five years, to see some of my senior students graduate. I had not seen any of them in person since the middle of March, when by state mandate we were all ordered to shelter in place. The administration and the parents did all they could to organize a meaningful virtual graduation for the students, a ceremony that stretched out for ten hours over two days. I arrived on the morning of the second day to watch a few of my favorite students receive their diplomas. The ceremonies took place on the football field. A group of ten students had an appointed time slot of fifteen minutes in which they walked onto the field, each standing under the assigned number from one to ten, socially distanced from each other. When Mike Ahn, the PE teacher known as "the voice of Northgate," announced the student's name, the student walked up to the central podium, there receiving a diploma and a handshake from the principal, and had two pictures taken, one alone and the other with family members who walked out to share the moment. Then each walked off, family in tow, back to their cars and drove away to whatever celebration awaited them with friends or at home. A handful of teachers sat in the bleachers, half-heartedly waving pompoms and cheering the students they knew. I stood at the fence by the field and waited to greet the students as they walked past after the picture-taking on the way to their cars. I offered my congratulations, talked briefly and warmly to those I knew best, and remained at least six feet away. Each fifteen minutes the procedure was replicated. After a couple of hours, I left to clean out my room for the summer.

That evening the school released on YouTube an hour-and-fifteen-minute video that included a short speech by a school board member, a faculty member's tribute to the class, student performances and speeches, and the introduction of students in the class of 2020 who received the class' highest honors. Then Mike Ahn read names and a picture of each graduate flashed on the screen. Everyone involved had the best of intentions and did the best they could under these circumstances. The product they turned out appeared professional and one of which they could be proud. But it all seemed forced, as I guess it had to be, and worse, joyless. I know, no matter how much virtual teaching I did, our school year ended two months before.

When we were told on March 13, 2020, that we were not returning to school, and that we were going to conduct classes virtually, everyone knew we were flying by the seat of our pants, and that we had to make things up as we went, venturing into this virtual world that many of us, particularly a technological dinosaur like me, knew little to nothing about. We had to learn the technology, try to determine what works, both technically and pedagogically, and what would be deemed legal in terms of equity and evaluation, and above all else try to figure out how to keep students engaged, particularly when innumerable forces of disengagement were working against us. We were neither prepared nor wise in how we implemented instruction for those two months; we did what we had to do under the circumstances. Students were less prepared, particularly emotionally, than we were—and many of them faced family and economic issues that we teachers knew nothing about that made a distanced schooling irrelevant. For several I know they learned hard financial lessons as for the first time they had to help provide for their families, others had to help parents fill out forms and documents for aid in a language in which only the child was proficient. School became irrelevant. We got through to the end, but I cannot say with any confidence that we did it successfully. Or that anyone learned anything— at least anything academic. We did learn that we lost a classroom that at times can feel like a family, a place to share joy and grief, accomplishment and loss. Many students lost a source of comfort with classmates and teachers who help them see the larger perspective, to let them know they were not alone.

Now the state, the school administrators and the teachers are all trying to invent a system from scratch. All of us are like the six blind men touching the elephant: we cannot see what part we are touching, and we have no idea what the whole animal looks like, so of course the animal looks deformed, as each of tries to patch together our individual sections. We know we must use distance learning before we know what it will look like. But those details and strategies of "distance learning" will be worked out—to one extent or another—because in our current environment they must be. The necessary focus will be on how we must do it, what are the effective "deliverables"? But what is not being asked at this time, perhaps because there are no immediate alternatives, is whether this distance learning is a good thing and how it will affect the ways and the models by which we can and should deliver education for the foreseeable future. As yet we know little about how social distancing and distance learning are connected, what elements they share, and what effects, perhaps devastating, they could have on learning and community, particularly in the humanities classroom.

To complicate matters even more, we are taking on this task when the fallout for the Covid pandemic has decimated projected budgets and funding. The issues of access and equity will undoubtedly lead to debates and lawsuits which will add more heat than light. At the same time the system will have to continue with fewer resources, making investments in infrastructure and professional development next to impossible. Technology and distanced learning might also be seen by many as a way to survive the economic devastation because after the initial investment they become relatively cheap. The gap between the have- and the have-nots most certainly will widen; those who are disenfranchised have one more valid reason to feel their disenfranchisement reinforced, and those who have been educationally privileged will punch one more ticket toward their future success. If test results and statistics reveal that basic skills can be taught remotely and successfully to those privileged who have always benefited by our educational system, I fear the move to some sort of permanent remote learning will gain momentum, and Betsy DeVos and the proponents of for-profit education will be there waiting to jump on that bandwagon and ride it all the way to the bank, having no consideration of the elements that define real education or what it means to actually touch children and prepare them for an uncertain future. One might be tempted to say, as I am, that along with "military intelligence" and "political integrity," "distance learning" will become one of the great modern oxymorons.

As we consider how we will blindly conceive this elephant that will become education, l want to return to the seniors I taught this year and what I feel are the unrecognized things we lost. An effective humanities classroom, and particularly an English classroom, is a community in which students share thoughts, share personal writings and experiences, take chances with each other. This process, as important as any skill they learn, takes time and patience—and it is a bumpy ride, accentuated Senior Year by the joy and fear the seniors feel at leaving. I have often observed that in spring semester of the senior year of high school, my students relive their entire educational careers. Sometime around April, as spring hits, they cannot pay attention, and they say they want to do nothing. Because they are aghast that we expect them to do anything at all, the simplest assignment perplexes them. They revert all the way to being giddy, silly, and rambunctious kindergarteners, possessing the attention spans of gnats. But if the class is successful, finally they come back when they realize that they are in fact leaving—it is not some distant dream of we've got to get out of this place, rather the stark realization that they are going to get out and that then things will be different, utterly. They become sober, reflective, caring for each other, their work, and the class. They recognize the community they created, and it becomes real for them and me. I believe that they come to see it as at least as important as anything else they have experienced in school. They take each other seriously. They care about the individual end-of-year projects that each of them produces and critique each other seriously and kindly. When they leave, they leave together—for the last time. Right now, we cannot touch that experience in a Zoom class—and I am not sure anyone who has experienced it believes that we ever will be able to—because it is next to impossible to touch them emotionally or physically.

This spring as our English Department met to discuss what obstacles we faced, no one mentioned anything about what we were teaching, only discussing how we were delivering the instruction. Perhaps this is inevitable as few of us had more than a clue of what we were doing. But in the midst of all this uncertainly, we must not lose sight of the purpose of the content we are teaching. A high school humanities curriculum is by definition the study of what makes us human, of what inspires us, touches us. So we must ask ourselves: how can we get to learn in this new environment? But more important, we must ask how can we reach out to the students? How can we make them feel these things? How do we touch their hearts? One thing we must not do is kid ourselves into believing that we are doing the same work and are doing it as effectively. We are not. All the methods I have learned to engage kids are impossible to use. The voice and inflection do not move them the same way, the stare does not penetrate. And one other way I know to reach students—the sense of touch—is now doubly verboten. I know teenagers like to be touched physically if it is done thoughtfully. This subject is threatening to all, particularly during this time of awareness of predators and disease. Some teachers who touch, and some who refuse to touch, should be nowhere near children, and of that we must always remain vigilant. Students read us as we read them, and they know teachers who like to touch and others do not. Intention matters, and most students know it intuitively. Because I am old, and comfortable doing it, I have been able, until now, to get away with patting students on the back, touching them on the shoulder, giving the occasional hug. When the touch is honest and respectful, students know we are present—that we care—when touch is caring and genuine, and when it is they relax physically and intellectually because they feel mutual trust, and most do not want to hide. On camera it is difficult enough to know if they are present let alone touch them—they can hide if they want to. Some have even learned how to put pictures of themselves on the screen to escape actually being there at all.

Then there is the energy students generate just by working together in the same room. There are days when I can feel the momentum build as they bounce ideas off each other in novel and sometimes goofy ways. Some goofy ideas may result in a high school *Medea*, or a satire of Donald Trump's decision-making process, or a slideshow illustrating Henry Reed's poem "The Naming of Parts." At these times there is laughter, there is joy. They have touched each other, and they are alive. The energy is contagious, and it cannot be passed through a video screen with each person in his or her own cubbyhole.

Last year I arrived at the opera ten minutes late for a production of Rossini's *The Barber of Seville*, and asked to wait in the lobby until intermission. A large TV monitor aired the production for latecomers, and my wife and I sat with three or four others watching on the screen what was going on on-stage. I sat there dazed, staring at the screen, hearing the voices, sealed in my own world; the actors and singers went through their motions as if underwater, and what would have electrified me in person, surrounded by other audience members, eliciting gasps and laughter, we greeted in deathly silence. There was no life, and we remained detached, unmoved. I imagined the singers performing in an empty auditorium, singing to no one, to silence. I turned to my wife and said, "Better not to be here at all." Two weeks later we returned and arrived on time to experience the opera from our seats. The opera was magnificent. Let us not become so jaded that we mistake a pale imitation of life, of art, for the real thing. So it must be in the classroom.

I will begin this fall semester with distanced learning with students whom I do not know and who do not know me. And now I am afraid. I am afraid I will not be able to what I have always been able to do, given the tools I know how to use. Mostly I am afraid that this marks a shift in education that may become irreversible, that we will settle for what we can do "remotely" and say that we have educated our children. Let us not pretend that what we are doing is the real thing and that it will suffice, because it does not. I will try my best to engage them, and some I know I will get to know and some I will reach. I will tell myself it is the best we can do in these unusual and trying times. I will adapt lessons accordingly to be provocative, use materials that speak to the current issues they face, find ways to elicit response that is not canned, where they can create and develop their voices on issues that matter. That is the job of a teacher, and it has not changed since the time of Socrates. Its methods and intent have not changed much in 2500 years. Now I am trying in front of TV screen to create life, to move people in real time, to touch their hearts as well as their minds, and bring about a sense of joy—and now I am afraid they will not in their seats, on their monitors, feel it.

We in education are not alone. I write about school because this is the field I know. Each of us is grappling with a sense of loss and a deep fear that the world has changed, and we do not yet know the magnitude nor understand the implications. I find it ironic that so many societal seismic eruptions, the pandemic being the most devastating, have taken place in the year 2020, *20/20* being a term when applied to vision means to see things clearly, and we must see clearly before we can imagine new strategies and implement thoughtful actions—in education and elsewhere. Albert Camus in *The Plague*, a novel that should be required reading at the moment, writes that good and evil do not really matter during a pandemic, or really any human crisis. "The evil in the world comes from ignorance, and good intentions may do as much harm as malevolence, if they lack understanding. On the whole men are more good than bad; that, however, isn't the real point. But they are more or less ignorant, and it is this that we call vice or virtue; the most incorrigible vice being that of an ignorance that fancies it knows everything and therefore claims for itself the right to kill." Only through banishing ignorance, and paying close attention to what we must do with the tool we have at hand can we persevere.

Still, I wish to remember Leila Okhravi, one of my students who walked out to receive her diploma while I stood along the football field that morning in June, wrote an email the following day. "I wanted to thank you for coming to my graduation yesterday! We were planning on having a lot more extended family over for the event but because of the circumstances, that didn't work out so it was nice to have someone else besides my immediate family there to watch me graduate." I showed up in person, and it touched her. That is the gift we have to give our students, to let them know that they touch us and that we can touch them. I never want to look back on what I have done, mourn the changes and the losses and say in resignation, "So it goes."

IT MADE ME WANT TO SING ALONG

UTTARA CHINTAMANI CHAUDHURI

During that week in March when Covid-19 went from being a something that happened in an elsewhere to a reality that was fast unravelling our lives, I felt especially dispirited about my upcoming creative writing workshops at Girls Inc. of Alameda County. I had been ridiculously excited about teaching this group of students—high-school seniors, all of them smart, ambitious women of color who were going to be taking a creative writing workshop for the first time. I was so enthusiastic that the risk management professional at UC Berkeley who had been appointed to conduct an orientation with the Simpson Fellows had to warn me to turn it down a notch. Gently, and with good humor, she suggested that I might consider fine-tuning my "love and hugs" energy to something closer to "platonic love and side-hugs." As I laughed that day, I could not have imagined a world in which a hug would become a disease-vector. Or that I would first encounter my students as animated pixels framed by tiny boxes on a computer screen.

I believed that teaching creative writing workshops was different than teaching almost anything else. Sharing one's writing with fellow students or an instructor is a big, scary, sacred thing. At minimum, it relies on a network of trust and a shared vocabulary for critical yet kind communication among the writers. And trust and communication, I was convinced, is built over time by writers who sit in the same room and slowly open up to one each other, not by those who briefly share screen-space. But despite my pessimism, I also knew that the only thing worse than a compromised experience would be for us to discontinue the program altogether.

So, with grim resignation, I opened a Zoom link on the day of our first class. After a round of introductions (I tried to memorize the names that bore little resemblance to their owners' quirky on-screen usernames), I began by asking the fifteen-or-so faces looking up from my computer screen whether the pandemic had at all altered their relationship with reading or writing. A few mentioned having more time for school-assigned writing assignments, one student said that her fanfiction was getting more lurid and another that the upheavals of quarantine had inspired a dream journal. Awkwardly, I tried to frame the situation. I told the scholars that I understood that our workshops were taking place in strange, unprecedented circumstances. As I chattered on nervously, the Junior Program Leader at Girls Inc., Carina Da Silva, typed into the small chat-box on the corner of the screen: "You're making history y'all !!!!." Instantly, the tiny boxes that housed our students lit up with their smiles. A little shiver ran through me; the eerie thought of passing into Capital-H-History but also, despite everything, the girls' infectious excitement had spilled over my computer screen.

It would be irresponsible to retrospectively romanticize the Zoom classroom. The circumstances were far from ideal. Transitioning online meant that we had fewer classes and reduced class-time. We assumed—rightly so I think—that students would be especially distracted and exhausted by increased screen exposure in already trying circumstances. But shorter, online classes meant that serious in-class writing and workshopping each other's work—which would have been essential components of the offline incarnation of this program—were no longer possible. Another unanticipated complication was the difficult demand an online classroom makes of us of being in front of a camera. Many students didn't want to turn their cameras on during class-time. I understood the impulse. Particularly for women, the world's ceaseless scrutiny on our bodies ensures that camera-shyness stays with most of us for a lifetime. And for women of color, our unease about our appearance is compounded by the relentless reminders that we will always be at a distance from the ideal of feminine beauty. Nonetheless, as instructors, we wanted our students to be on a level field and so requested that they show their faces to us. But I realized quickly that the field would never be level. You are an interloper when you can look into one student's messy room with the curtains still drawn and then another's with sunlight streaming in and motivational wall-posters—and you make snap judgments. You have to remind yourself not to.

For all its difficulties, however, the online classroom also pushed some interesting pedagogical choices. I realized, for instance, that if I needed to introduce poetry or fiction writing in an hour over Zoom, rules were at once essential and secondary. That is, I was perhaps excessively programmatic on the one hand—spending a lot of time on things like rhyme schemes or story-telling roadmaps (A is for action, B is for background…). We needed concrete tools that could be written down and committed to memory. However, precisely because of my anxiety about an overreliance on these methods, I wanted my students to know that they must control their craft, not be controlled by it. So at the end of every class, I reminded them that the techniques we had just spent the last half-hour discussing were not so important after all. The important thing was to access that raw, vulnerable place inside us from which we say something that matters. Then we could use the rules or break them or make new rules—but intentionally, and in our most honest voice. I find myself wondering whether I would have emphasized this approach—or rather, learnt this lesson—with my students in different circumstances.

In the second week of class, we set out do a poem-building exercise as an icebreaker. I started with a line and each scholar was to add one of their own. The idea was to try and instinctively find our poetic feet without thinking too much or letting our inner critic take over. Perhaps unsurprisingly, in both the morning and afternoon sessions of the workshop, the scholars wrote about the pandemic. And in both groups, these tag-along-lines accumulated to create what felt, unmistakably, like poems; managing (approximate meter notwithstanding) to achieve rhythm and a certain coherence of feeling. Take the following verse about the experience of indoor isolation: *The birds chirped different songs / It made me want to sing along / Passing through the long halls / I thought of life beyond these walls.*

Four lines, written in mere minutes by four scholars from the isolation of their homes. It felt like a Covid miracle. As one of my students said at the end of class, "I feel less alone now. There's just something about knowing that someone else is going through what you are."

On the day of our final class, we looked back at our experience of the workshops and then forward, as we talked about the upcoming college admissions cycle. All my students want to go to college. They, like students everywhere, are excited by the sheer range of possibilities that lie before them but scared by the prospect of rejection. Yet as women of color, their experience is particular and of course, one of my incisive students put her finger right on it. As scholars shared their take-aways from the workshop, she said that what she had appreciated most was that our classroom had become a safe space for students to discuss their daily encounters with micro-aggressions. "You don't even feel like blaming individuals," she said, "when there's a whole system that's putting you down every day." A "hmm" of understanding went around the screen; almost all the students who spoke after her echoed the sentiment. My students are aware that the stakes of the college application (and every other application) are higher for them, that their achievements are more hard-won. The daily fight against the "whole system," at once all-encompassing and insidious, can be exhausting. Yet perhaps there is some comfort to be had, if momentarily, in being able to talk about your anxieties with those who share and therefore fully understand them.

Through the course of our workshops, we had read many stories, poems and memoirs by women of color. As we broke texts down and then thought about what held them together, we had talked about why a writer used the formal device she did to articulate a particular experience of oppression, or how she could use language to evoke a range of emotional effects around a single incident. Yet until that moment, it hadn't struck me how much those discussions had created a network of solidarity among our group of Black, Latina, Asian, and Indian women. But perhaps that's the thing about stories—reading them, talking about them, writing them— they have a way of bringing people together even under the most absurd circumstances.

I began my workshops convinced that teaching creative writing was uniquely ill-suited to the online transition that the pandemic had forced us to make. Instead, my time with the scholars at Girls Inc. taught me that stories alone can, and always have, defied social distancing. Good stories foster radical empathy so that we can inhabit the minds and hearts of those far from us, even as they remind us of how much we have in common.

My colleague was right—the scholars at Girls Inc. made history. I don't know if they came to the workshops willingly, under the circumstances, but I do know that they discovered their best writing selves in spite of them. This group of women refused to let the anxieties of the pandemic dull either their creative instincts or their work ethic. Instead, each of my students both drew from our workshops and surpassed its teachings. As the pieces in this anthology demonstrate, they did the brave and difficult work of travelling deep inside themselves and then finding the language to put their thoughts into words and words onto paper. When they look back on this tumultuous moment in the years to come, I do hope that the scholars at Girls Inc. will be very proud of themselves. For they used the time that was made available to them as they sheltered-in-place to do the thing which not only helps us survive crises but feel alive every day—they listened to others' stories and had the courage to tell their own.

POST-(MOVIE)-SCRIPT

SHAKESPEARE & THE PLAGUE

PHILIPPA KELLY & JOSEPH DI PRISCO

The Simpson Literary Project presents Shakespeare & the Plague. Shakespeare lived his entire life in the shadow of a plague, and his plays reference dread familiar to us during our own pandemic. Pulitzer Prize-winner Stephen Greenblatt of Harvard University, General Editor of The Norton Shakespeare, introduces this mash-up curated by Philippa Kelly and performed by the Pandemic Popup Players. Filmed by Obatala Mawusi and Fox Nakai at the California Shakespeare Theater. Music by Paul Dresher. Directed by Philippa Kelly. Produced by Joseph Di Prisco.

> *"Shakespeare lived his whole life in the shadow of the plague. The plague is present as a steady undertone throughout his plays, surfacing most often in expressions of disgust or rage or self-loathing. Shakespeare struck this disturbing note in words that were meant to be performed before thousands of people, all of whose lives had been overturned as ours have been by the plague."*
> — Stephen Greenblatt

ACTOR ONE

WE SHALL ALL BE MASKED! All call out: LOVE'S LABOUR'S LOST!!

Welcome everybody. I am Master of the Prologue and, occasionally, Prince of Time, stepping in to offer commentary on the trivial subjects of life and mortality.

Let's get started. You all know the Tragedy of *Romeo and Juliet*, right? Well, if you only knew it better, you'd see that it's the tragedy of ME. I only just get going and they take me off stage, replacing me with those two love-drunk ingenues. What do they know of love? I can tell you about love, believe me, in ALL its iterations. I mean, why do those two even *need* to come on at all?

> *Two households, both alike in dignity,*
> *In fair Verona, where we lay our scene,*
> *From ancient grudge break to new mutiny,*
> *Where civil blood makes civil hands unclean.*
> *From forth the fatal loins of these two foes*
> *A pair of star-cross'd lovers take their life;*
> *Whose misadventured piteous overthrows*
> *Do with their death bury their parents' strife.*
> *The fearful passage of their death-mark'd love,*
> *And the continuance of their parents' rage,*
> *Which, but their children's end, nought could remove,*
> *Is now the two hours' traffic of our stage;*
> *The which if you with patient ears attend,*
> *What here shall miss, our toil shall strive to mend.*

BREAK

PHILIPPA: By the time Shakespeare wrote these words in about 1594, the plague had repeatedly invaded his world—the first time when the playwright was only three months old. The bubonic plague had horrible symptoms: fever, breathlessness, body pain, insatiable thirst—and then buboes, or large, hard plague sores in the groin, armpits, or neck, that would rupture and cause such excruciating pain that some diseased citizens would leap from windows to escape the agony. Those aged ten to thirty-five were especially vulnerable, and youth and strong bodies did NOT spare them from the worst symptoms of the plague.

Because no one knew then what caused the bubonic plague, it was very difficult to contain the spread. And the only treatment folks had was to shut up a plague-infected house (in *Romeo and Juliet* I made it— well, *Shakespeare* made it—a useful plot point to keep Friar John from delivering a crucial letter).

And of course the plague spread in the language of the period— Just as Covid-related language has spread today—as in *self-isolating, infodemic, shelter-in-place, elbow-bump.*

In Shakespeare's time the physical symptoms of the plague were used as noxious metaphors for infectious attitudes and beliefs. Did you notice the moment back there when I said "their death-marked love?" Just as the plague marked citizens for death, Romeo and Juliet's love is "death-marked" by the "plague" of their parents' long-held toxic rivalry. I could've told them that, if only they hadn't cut me off at the prologue.

Well, Master of the Prologue, I know you've seen it all before: but although the story of love is old, YOU can't LIVE it. Every single lover is unique, every single love, wrestles with the story of love, peril, disappointment, agony—all those elemental emotions—in their own way. You talk about being cut off at the prologue—but *who has ever cut off a passionate embrace because YOU warn them that they won't feel that way forever?*

ACTOR ONE: Let me get a word in here. I'm just bringing in a much-needed dose of history and reality. Just like Mercutio does before his death in *Romeo and Juliet*. Mercutio uses the mortal force of the plague to make folks *feel* the infection of hatred that has already caused death in the play and will cause more: "A plague on both your houses," he says. And in his dying words, as he repeats, "A plague on both your houses," he curses with the plague the very two family houses whose toxic energy is responsible for his death.

Yep, Mercutio nailed that one.

The imagery of illness and death—the perils of a corrupting feud that weakens those born in its shadow—is also an underscore for the teenagers' framing of their love in *Romeo and Juliet*:

ACTOR TWO
ROMEO
Bid a sick man in sadness make his will:
Ah, word ill urged to one that is so ill!
But, soft! what light through yonder window breaks?
It is the east, and Juliet is the sun.
Arise, fair sun, and kill the envious moon,
Who is already sick and pale with grief,

That thou her maid art far more fair than she:
Be not her maid, since she is envious;
Her vestal livery is but sick and green
And none but fools do wear it; cast it off.

And Juliet wants to free her new love, Romeo, from the contagion of their parents' fight—whose cause is so long forgotten that only the names "Capulet" and "Montague" remain as gateways to the poisonous family feud:

ACTOR THREE

Tis but thy name that is my enemy;
Thou art thyself, though not a Montague.
What's Montague? it is nor hand, nor foot,
Nor arm, nor face, nor any other part
Belonging to a man. O, be some other name!
What's in a name? that which we call a rose
By any other name would smell as sweet;
So Romeo would, were he not Romeo call'd,
Retain that dear perfection which he owes
Without that title. Romeo, doff thy name,
And for that name which is no part of thee
Take all myself.

BREAK

ACTOR ONE: Ah—oh, that brings a tear to even my jaded eye…! Let's move along, let's change the tempo… Shakespeare also used London's plague-ridden air as a symbol of inner corruption—a corruption of the soul. Listen to Portia's words in Julius Caesar.

ACTOR THREE

What, is Brutus sick?
And will he steal out of his wholesome bed,
To dare the vile contagion of the night
And tempt the rheumy and unpurged air
To add unto his sickness? No, my Brutus;
You have some sick offence within your mind…"

ACTOR ONE: In the world of politics and greed, ill-gotten ambition can poison the mind and destroy the soul, whether it be ancient Rome, Shakespeare's London, or 2020s America.

BREAK

PHILIPPA: Listen also to this passage from *King Lear*. You'll notice that Lear weeps about his heartless daughters and calls them monstrous carbuncles—for him they're metaphorical embodiments of the ghastly plague, with its ugliness and pain.

ACTOR TWO as Lear:
I prithee, daughter, do not make me mad:
I will not trouble thee, my child; farewell:
We'll no more meet, no more see one another:
But yet thou art my flesh, my blood, my daughter;
Or rather a disease that's in my flesh,
Which I must needs call mine: thou art a boil,
A plague-sore, an embossed carbuncle,
In my corrupted blood.

ACTOR ONE: Can you imagine a father today describing his teenager as an embodiment of Covid-19? You'd feel pretty bad to hear that. Well, guess what? Lear's daughters don't love him for his curses! And things don't go well for Lear, you won't be surprised to hear.

BREAK

PHILIPPA: That's not the only reference to the plague in *King Lear*. The dreadful disease is also used to describe a stroke of fate sent by the heavens—humbling humans in their fruitless wish to control the ruthless hand of fate: Here's Gloucester with his son Edgar. Near the top of the play, Edgar's brother Edmund has persuaded their father that Edgar has wanted him dead. With only the evidence of a forged letter, Gloucester has jumped to believe Edmund, pursuing the loyal Edgar as a criminal. Now Edgar, good man that he is, has come back disguised as a beggar to help his father, whom Edmund and his friends Goneril, Regan, and Cornwall, have blinded and cast out. Listen to Gloucester speaking of **the**

heaven's plague that has humbled him. He uses the plague as a metaphor for the wretched fate that fortune has plagued him with.

ACTOR THREE: GLOUCESTER

Know'st thou the way to Dover?

ACTOR TWO: EDGAR

Both stile and gate, horse-way and footpath. Poor
Tom hath been scared out of his good wits: bless
thee, good man's son, from the foul fiend! five
fiends have been in poor Tom at once; of lust, as
Obidicut; Hobbididence, prince of dumbness; Mahu, of
stealing; Modo, of murder; Flibbertigibbet, of
mopping and mowing, who since possesses chambermaids
and waiting-women. So, bless thee, master!

ACTOR THREE: GLOUCESTER

Here, take this purse, thou whom the heavens' plagues
Have humbled to all strokes: that I am wretched
Makes thee the happier: heavens, deal so still!
Let the superfluous and lust-dieted man,
That slaves your ordinance, that will not see
Because he doth not feel, feel your power quickly;
So distribution should undo excess,
And each man have enough. Dost thou know Dover?

ACTOR TWO: EDGAR

Ay, master.

ACTOR THREE: GLOUCESTER

There is a cliff, whose high and bending head
Looks fearfully in the confined deep:
Bring me but to the very brim of it,
And I'll repair the misery thou dost bear
With something rich about me: from that place
I shall no leading need.

ACTOR TWO: EDGAR

Give me thy arm:
Poor Tom shall lead thee.
[Incredible compassion in this exchange]

BREAK

ACTOR ONE: And when we look at another play, *Macbeth*, we see Shakespeare using the plague metaphor to describe a corruption of the whole world: wrought not by the heavens, as Gloucester sees it in *King Lear*, but by two characters who have embraced immorality:

ACTOR TWO:

Alas, poor country,
Almost afraid to know itself. It cannot
Be called our mother, but our grave, where nothing
But who knows nothing is once seen to smile;
Where sighs and groans and shrieks that rend the air
Are made, not marked; where violent sorrow seems
A modern ecstasy. The dead man's knell
Is there scarce asked for who, and good men's lives
Expire before the flowers in their caps,
Dying or ere they sicken.

ACTOR ONE: Near the close of the play, Lady Macbeth's hands literally "embody" the corruption that she and her husband have wrought on the entire world of Scotland. They've infected the whole world, and the tortured Lady Macbeth sees her hands as "spotted" by the plague of her own moral corruption.

ACTOR ONE: Doctor

What is it she does now? Look, how she rubs her hands.

ACTOR TWO: Gentlewoman

It is an accustomed action with her, to seem thus
washing her hands: I have known her continue in
this a quarter of an hour.

ACTOR THREE: LADY MACBETH

Yet here's a spot.

DOCTOR

*Hark! she speaks: I will set down what comes from
her, to satisfy my remembrance the more strongly.*

LADY MACBETH

*Out, damned spot! out, I say!—One: two: why,
then, 'tis time to do't.—Hell is murky!—Fie, my
lord, fie! a soldier, and afeard? What need we
fear who knows it, when none can call our power to
account?—Yet who would have thought the old man
to have had so much blood in him.*

DOCTOR

Do you mark that?

LADY MACBETH

*The thane of Fife had a wife: where is she now?—
What, will these hands ne'er be clean?—No more o'
that, my lord, no more o' that: you mar all with
this starting.*

DOCTOR

Go to, go to; you have known what you should not.

ACTOR TWO (Gentlewoman)

*She has spoke what she should not, I am sure of
that: heaven knows what she has known.*

LADY MACBETH

*Here's the smell of the blood still: all the
perfumes of Arabia will not sweeten this little
hand. Oh, oh, oh!*

ACTOR ONE: And Lady Macbeth's fall is echoed soon thereafter. "The
mind I sway by and the heart I bear/Shall never sag with doubt nor shake

with fear," cries her husband, resisting his demise with all the strength of will and superstition.

Macbeth trusts the witch's words, "Macbeth shall never vanquish'd be until/Great Birnam wood to high Dunsinane hill/Shall come against him." Yet Birnam wood *does* rise to Dunsinane. Plagues cruelly toy with us, too, when we don't take them seriously. *Actor One hamming up the school teacher voice here:* Shall we break into small groups and discuss irony, everyone?

BREAK

ACTOR TWO: But the plague isn't always a tragic emblem: characters also joke about it, much as we might today:

In *Much Ado* Beatrice says of Benedick, trying to hide her love for him:

ACTOR THREE:

O Lord! He will hang upon him like a disease. He is sooner caught than the pestilence, and the taker runs presently mad. God help the noble Claudio. If he have caught the Benedict it will cost him a thousand pound ere 'a be cured.

BREAK

ACTOR THREE: And humor can be mashed up with cheerful resignation, as when the countess Olivia in *Twelfth Night* marvels at the speed with which she's fallen in love:

How now?
Even so quickly may one catch the plague?
Methinks I feel this youth's perfections
With an invisible and subtle stealth
To creep in at mine eyes. Well, let it be.

ACTOR ONE:

And yes, you got it, the plague, lingering and horribly infectious as it might be, is not always a downer. *The Tempest* suggests that we can purge ourselves of infectious, negative thoughts just like purging ourselves of disease. That's cheering, isn't it? Even if we can't get rid of the physical plague, at least we can leave this life with a plague-free mind.

Prospero is cursed by Caliban: "The Red Plague catch thee/For learning me your language," Prospero is so dismissive of Caliban, his slave, that he never even thinks about what Caliban's curse means. Prospero is so busy listening to the story in his *own* head that he can't hear Caliban. Old man Prospero has cast a plague of sorts on Caliban, imprisoning him and condemning him to servitude—Prospero assumes that he has the right to do so. But at the end of the play he learns how to let go, and this is a beautiful moment. Yes, he releases Caliban, he releases everyone on the island. And, what is really amazing, he releases HIMSELF from the perseverant revenge drama that he has planned and executed.

Philippa, I love this, because Shakespeare suggests that if we can release ourselves from the chains and plaguesores of resentment, we can transcend. We can be free. We can have a second chance at life.

BREAK

ACTOR TWO

> Ye elves of hills, brooks, standing lakes and groves,
> And ye that on the sands with printless foot
> Do chase the ebbing Neptune and do fly him
> When he comes back; you demi-puppets that
> By moonshine do the green sour ringlets make,
> Whereof the ewe not bites, and you whose pastime
> Is to make midnight mushrooms, that rejoice
> To hear the solemn curfew; by whose aid,
> Weak masters though ye be, I have bedimm'd
> The noontide sun, call'd forth the mutinous winds,
> And 'twixt the green sea and the azured vault
> Set roaring war: to the dread rattling thunder
> Have I given fire and rifted Jove's stout oak
> With his own bolt; the strong-based promontory
> Have I made shake and by the spurs pluck'd up
> The pine and cedar: graves at my command
> Have waked their sleepers, oped, and let 'em forth
> By my so potent art. But this rough magic
> I here abjure, and, when I have required
> Some heavenly music, which even now I do,

> *To work mine end upon their senses that*
> *This airy charm is for, I'll break my staff,*
> *Bury it certain fathoms in the earth,*
> *And deeper than did ever plummet sound*
> *I'll drown my book.*

BREAK

ACTOR ONE

> *Now my charms are all o'erthrown,*
> *And what strength I have's mine own,*
> *Which is most faint: now, 'tis true,*
> *I must be here confined by you,*
> *Or sent to Naples. Let me not,*
> *Since I have my dukedom got*
> *And pardon'd the deceiver, dwell*
> *In this bare island by your spell;*
> *But release me from my bands*
> *With the help of your good hands:*
> *Gentle breath of yours my sails*
> *Must fill, or else my project fails,*
> *Which was to please. Now I want*
> *Spirits to enforce, art to enchant,*
> *And my ending is despair,*
> *Unless I be relieved by prayer,*
> *Which pierces so that it assaults*
> *Mercy itself and frees all faults.*
> *As you from crimes would pardon'd be,*
> *Let your indulgence set me free.*

~

Viewer's Guide

Background information and discussion questions for teaching *Shakespeare & the Plague* in class and on stage. Composed by Director and Dramaturg Philippa Kelly.

https://www.simpsonliteraryproject.org/shakespeare-and-the-plague

CONTRIBUTORS

Michelle Alas (she/her) is a senior at Northgate High School in the San Francisco Bay Area and a lover of reading, writing, and running. As a Salvadoran-American, Michelle enjoys writing about her culture and her family. Michelle is a strong advocate for education equity and social justice, and will be attending Brown University in the Fall of 2021.

Shanti Ariker is an attorney and currently General Counsel at Zendesk in San Francisco. Shanti was chosen as one of ten lucky participants for a Simpson Literary Project workshop with Joyce Carol Oates. This story was a result of the work done in the workshop and, as a result, Shanti continues to work on her memoir and has joined the board of the Project, which she is thrilled to contribute to, having seen the benefit of the programming for herself. She lives in Northern California with her husband and twins. She attended Hebrew University and University of Massachusetts at Boston before going to law school at University of Virginia.

Originally from New Delhi, India, **Uttara Chintamani Chaudhuri** is a second-year graduate student in the English Department at the University of California, Berkeley. When she is not reading, writing, or teaching, she likes to daydream, take long walks, exchange bad puns, listen to music, cook, and, occasionally, sing. She is a Simpson Fellow.

Grace Decker, a graduate of Northgate High School, is a college student in Vermont.

Joseph Di Prisco is Founding Chair of the Simpson Literary Project and author or editor of sixteen books, including fiction, prize-winning poetry, memoir, and nonfiction. His most recent works include *Sightlines from the Cheap Seats* (his third book of poetry; 2017), *The Pope of Brooklyn* (his second memoir; 2017), and *The Good Family Fitzgerald* (his sixth novel; 2020). He grew up in Brooklyn and Berkeley. He received his PhD from UC Berkeley, and has taught English and creative writing, from middle school through college and beyond. He has also served as Trustee or Chair of several nonprofit boards devoted to education, the arts, theater, and children's mental health. Forthcoming is a book of short stories.

Asha Dunn is seventeen and a senior at Oakland Technical High School. She is in the Graphic Design Academy there and so has a lot of interest in the arts. She loves music and has learned to play multiple instruments. She also values environmental awareness and has participated in many clean-ups in her city. She looks forward to where these interests might take her in the future.

Izba Haq is an upcoming senior at San Leandro High School. One of her goals for the future is to pursue a career in the medical field, such as nursing, and possibly run her own clothing/cosmetics business on the side. She hopes to be stable, both mentally and financially, and to view her career as an interest rather than as a job.

Maria Dahvana Headley is the *New York Times*-bestselling author of *The Mere Wife*, a contemporary adaptation of *Beowulf*, named by the *Washington Post* as one of its Notable Works of Fiction in 2018. Her new translation of *Beowulf* was published by FSG in August 2020. She has published three previous novels, including *Queen of Kings* and YA novels *Magonia* and *Aerie*. With Neil Gaiman, she edited the anthology *Unnatural Creatures* to benefit 826DC, and with Kat Howard, she wrote *The End of the Sentence*, one of NPR's Best Books of 2014. Her internationally bestselling memoir, *The Year of Yes*, was published in more than a dozen languages. Headley's short fiction has been nominated for the Nebula, Shirley Jackson, Tiptree, and World Fantasy Awards and has been anthologized in many year's bests; a collection will appear from FSG in the near future. Her essays on politics, propaganda, and mythology have been published in *The New York Times, The Daily Beast,* Harvard's *Nieman Storyboard*, and elsewhere. Her work has been supported by The MacDowell Colony, Arte Studio Ginestrelle, and the Sundance Institute's Theatre Lab, among other organizations. She grew up in the high desert of

Idaho on a survivalist sled dog ranch, where she spent summers plucking the winter coat from her father's wolf.

Jasmin Jacobo is a rising senior at Oakland Charter High School. She enjoys spending her time going on hikes, reading, and having family time. She aspires to become a businesswoman.

T. Geronimo Johnson was the 2017 Simpson/Joyce Carol Oates Prize Recipient. He was born in New Orleans, is a graduate of the Iowa Writers' Workshop. A former Stegner Fellow, Johnson has taught at UC Berkeley, Stanford, the Writers' Workshop, the Prague Summer Program, OSU, TSU, San Quentin, and elsewhere. He has worked on, at, or in brokerages, kitchens, construction sites, phone rooms, education nonprofits, writing centers, summer camps, ladies shoe stores, nightclubs, law firms, offset print shops, and a political campaign that shall remain unnamed. He also wrote a couple of novels that have—between the two—been selected by the Wall Street Journal Book Club, named a 2013 PEN/Faulkner Award finalist, shortlisted for the 2016 Hurston Wright Legacy Award, longlisted for the National Book Award, longlisted for the Andrew Carnegie Medal for Excellence in Fiction, a finalist for The Bridge Book Award, a finalist for the Mark Twain American Voice in Literature Award, included on Time Magazine's list of the top ten books of 2015, awarded the Saroyan International Prize for Writing, named the winner of the 2015 Ernest J Gaines Award for Literary Excellence, and the inaugural Simpson Family Literary Prize (now known as The Simpson/Joyce Carol Oates Prize). Johnson was a 2016 National Book Award judge. He is a Fellow of the American Academy in Rome, and currently resides in the Eternal City. http://www.geronimo1.com/

Amira Jourdan is a rising senior at Holy Names High School. She is involved in a number of extracurricular activities at her school, such as Student Council, Black Student Union (BSU), and golf. On the weekends she works a part-time job at a local bakery in Oakland, where she is able to express her creativity. She plans to attend college next year and later enter a career in the STEAM field.

Philippa Kelly (PhD Shakespeare) is Resident Dramaturg for the California Shakespeare Theater. A Fulbright, Rockefeller, Walter and

Eliza Hall, and Commonwealth Scholar, and co-recipient of a Literary Managers and Dramaturgs of the Americas Bly Award for Innovation in Dramaturgy, Philippa has published twelve books and ninety-six articles. Philippa's Arden book, *The King and I* illuminates *King Lear* through the lens of Australia's history of outcasting. Her *Run the Canon* series at Cal Shakes presents original twelve-minute video talks on Shakespeare's canon, https://calshakes.org/cal-shakes-online/run-the-canon/. Philippa is dedicated to teaching, and over several years, Philippa has led Walter and Elise Haas and California Arts Council-funded teams to bring curriculum components into under-funded schools across the Bay. She leads a year-round community theater appreciation group entitled *Berkeley Theater Explorations*. At present she is dramaturging *Macbeth* for Laney College and *Henry V* for the African American Shakespeare Company.

Laila Lalami was the 2019 Simpson/Joyce Carol Oates Prize Recipient. She born in Rabat and educated in Morocco, Great Britain, and the United States. She is the author of the novels *Hope and Other Dangerous Pursuits*, which was a finalist for the Oregon Book Award; *Secret Son*, which was on the Orange Prize longlist; and *The Moor's Account*, which won the American Book Award, the Arab American Book Award, and the Hurston/Wright Legacy Award. It was on the Man Booker Prize longlist and was a finalist for the Pulitzer Prize. Her essays and opinion pieces have appeared in the *Los Angeles Times*, the *Washington Post*, *The Nation*, *Harper's*, the *Guardian*, and the *New York Times*. She writes the "Between the Lines" column for *The Nation* magazine and is a critic-at-large for the *Los Angeles Times*. The recipient of a British Council Fellowship, a Fulbright Fellowship, and a Guggenheim Fellowship, she is currently a professor of creative writing at the University of California at Riverside. Her latest novel, *The Other Americans*, was published by Pantheon in March 2019, and was a finalist for the National Book Award. lailalalami.com

Olivia Loscavio is a nineteen-year-old Bay Area native, a graduate of Northgate High School, and a freshman at Occidental College. She has been creative writing since her early teens and began her literary journey with the Simpsonistas workshop two years ago. She likes writing about the miracles and tragedies of everyday life, and writes to build a cohesive view of her environment and herself. Lately, her work has been focusing on the way the identities she was raised with clash and come together with the identities she has developed through becoming her own woman.

Ian S. Maloney is Professor of Literature, Writing, and Publishing at St. Francis College in Brooklyn, NY. Ian serves on the Literary Council for the Brooklyn Book Festival and as Community Outreach Director for the Walt Whitman Initiative. He recently completed his first novel, *South Brooklyn Exterminating*.

Ngalifourou Matingou, aka "Ngali," seventeen, is of Congolese (Central African) Heritage, born and raised in Oakland, CA. She currently attends Visions in Education Charter School and is enrolled in their University Prep program. She has been dancing ever since she was born and has performed with a few dance companies studying forms such as Haitian, Congolese, and Contemporary dance. Some other interests include swimming, gymnastics, photography, and cooking. Her passion is Culinary Arts, and she aspires to become a professional Chef. She is concurrently enrolled in the Culinary Arts program at Laney College in Oakland, CA. Her dream is to attend a (HBCU) Historically Black College and University to pursue a Business Degree in Entrepreneurship to compliment her interest in the Culinary Arts.

Daniel Mason is a physician and author of *The Piano Tuner* (2002), *A Far Country* (2007), *The Winter Soldier* (2018), and *A Registry of My Passage Upon the Earth* (2020). His work has been translated into twenty-eight languages, awarded the Northern California Book Award for Fiction, and shortlisted for the James Tait Black Memorial Prize. *The Piano Tuner* was produced as an opera by Music Theatre Wales, and adapted to the stage by Lifeline Theatre. His short stories and essays have appeared in *Harper's*, *Zoetrope: All Story and Lapham's Quarterly*; in 2014 he was a recipient of a fellowship from the National Endowment for the Arts. A Clinical Assistant Professor in the Stanford University Department of Psychiatry, his research and teaching interests include the subjective experience of mental illness and the influence of literature, history, and culture on the practice of medicine.

Regan McMahon is Deputy Editor, Books, at Common Sense Media, a nonprofit website that helps kids, parents, and educators navigate the world of media and technology. She's a member of the National Book Critics Circle, the copy editor for the San Francisco literary journal *Zyzzyva*, and a freelance book editor of fiction and nonfiction. Previously a book critic, feature writer, and Deputy Book Editor at the *San Francisco Chronicle*, she's also the author of *Revolution in the Bleachers* (Gotham/Viking).

Joyce Carol Oates is Joyce Carol Oates. She was the Simpson Project Writer-in-Residence at the Lafayette Library and Learning Center (2018, 2019), and is an honorary member of the Simpson Literary Project Board. She was the Roger S. Berlind Distinguished Professor of the Humanities at Princeton University, where she continues to teach, and has been the recipient of numerous awards, including the National Book Award, the PEN/Malamud Award for Excellence in Short Fiction, the 2019 Jerusalem Prize, and the 2020 The Cino del Duca World Prize. She is the prolific author of novels, short stories, memoirs, poetry, and nonfiction; and, as legions of readers around the world appreciate, an author of unparalleled range, depth, and accomplishment. Her most recent books are *Night; Sleep; Death; The Stars;* and *Cardiff, By the Sea*. Her advice to writers is profoundly simple: "Write your heart out."

JoAnne Ohwobete is a rising senior at Moreau Catholic High School in Hayward California. She enjoys playing volleyball, hanging out with family, and hopes to pursue a degree in psychology in the future.

Chicago-born **Peter Orner** is the author of five books of fiction, including the novels *The Second Coming of Mavala Shikongo* (2006) and *Love and Shame and Love* (2010), and the story collections, *Esther Stories* (2001, 2013, with a new foreword by Marilynne Robinson), *Last Car Over the Sagamore Bridge* (2013), and most recently, *Maggie Brown & Others* (2019). Orner's essay collection, *Am I Alone Here?: Notes on Reading to Live and Living to Read* (2016) was a National Book Critics Circle Award finalist. He is also the editor of three books of oral history for the Voice of Witness series, *Underground America* (2008), *Hope Deferred: Narratives of Zimbabwean Lives* (2011), and *Lavil: Life, Love, and Death in Port-*

au-Prince (2017). His stories and essays have appeared in the *Atlantic Monthly, The New Yorker, The New York Times, Granta, The Believer,* and the *Paris Review,* as well as in *Best American Short Stories.* Orner has received Guggenheim and Lannan Foundation fellowships, a California Book Award, the Edward Lewis Wallant Award for Jewish Writing, and three Pushcart Prizes. Orner is a Professor of English and Creative Writing at Dartmouth College and lives with his family in Norwich, Vermont.

Dallas Panopio is currently a senior at San Leandro High School. In her free time, she likes to read books, write stories of her own, and paint. Her dream is to one day become a successful TV/movie director.

Esmeralda Pedroza is currently an incoming senior at Bishop O'Dowd High School. Her hobbies are writing, meeting new people, and doing whatever she can to help others. Her aspirations are to go to a four-year college, graduate, and be in one of the following three professions: medical, business, or finance. She hopes you enjoy her writing and get to know her a bit more!

Anne Raeff's new novel, *Only the River,* was published by Counterpoint in May 2020 and has been long-listed for the 2020 Simpson/Joyce Carol Oates Prize and listed by the *Chicago Review of Books* as one of eleven Must-Read Books of the Month. Her second novel, *Winter Kept Us Warm,* published in 2018, won the silver medal for the California Book Award for Fiction. Her short story collection, *The Jungle Around Us* won the 2015 Flannery O'Connor Award for Short Fiction. The collection was also a finalist for the California Book Award and was on *The San Francisco Chronicle's* 100 Best Books of 2017 list. In 2019 she was a finalist for the Joyce Carol Oates Prize. Clara Mondschein's *Melancholia,* also a novel, was published in 2002. Raeff's stories and essays have appeared in *New England Review, ZYZZYVA,* and *Guernica* among other places. She is proud to be a high school teacher and lives in San Francisco.

Michael Ross is a member of the board of directors of the Simpson Literary Project. He earned his BA with distinction (1970) and his JD (1977) from the University of Virginia. He ended his career in the Navy as a Lieutenant and Operations Officer of the USS Truckee. He was a corporate lawyer, specializing in mergers and acquisitions, at Latham & Watkins and later served as Senior Vice President and General Counsel at Safeway Inc. He was a visiting lecturer at the University of Virginia and Berkeley Schools of Law, Peking University's School of Transnational Law, Dubrovnik International University, and the IE Law School in Madrid. He and his wife, Virginia, live in Orinda, California, and have a son, Charlie (25), and a daughter, Margaret (23).

Morgan Vincent lives in San Leandro, CA and is a senior at Bishop O'Dowd High School. At Bishop O'Dowd, Morgan is an executive member of the Black Student Union and Student Council and participates in Varsity Cheer. In college, Morgan plans to pursue a major in biological sciences with a minor in writing and music theory. After graduation, Morgan plans to attend medical school and pursue a career in dermatology.

Noah Warren is the recipient of the Yale Series of Younger Poets (*The Destroyer in the Glass* [2016]) and a Wallace Stegner Fellowship. His next book, *The Complete Stories,* will be published by Copper Canyon Press in 2021. He is pursuing a PhD in the UC Berkeley English Department. He was a Simpson Fellow in 2020 and will be a Simpson Fellow in 2021.

David Wood has taught English at Northgate High School since 1984, and is a member of the Simpson Literary Project Board; he also served on the jury for the Joyce Carol Oates Prize. He was a board member and board president of the celebrated Aurora Theatre Company, and now serves on the Advisory Board for the Kalmanovitz School of Education at Saint Mary's College of California. A Yale graduate and University of Chicago MA, he estimates he is coming up on his hundredth year of teaching.

Simpson Literary Project

Please support students, teachers, writers, and readers.

To donate to our 501(c)3 nonprofit, go to our website:

simpsonliteraryproject.org

Or contact Diane Del Signore, Executive Director

diane@simpsonliteraryproject.org

Thank you. Your generosity makes all the difference.

CPSIA information can be obtained
at www.ICGtesting.com
Printed in the USA
LVHW042336130421
684424LV00002B/2

9 781644 282250